Cope with Change at W

Sue Stockdale and Clive Steeper

Teach
Yourself

Cope with Change at Work

Sue Stockdale and Clive Steeper

Hodder Education
338 Euston Road, London NW1 3BH.

Hodder Education is an Hachette UK company

First published in UK 2012 by Hodder Education

First published in US 2012 by The McGraw-Hill Companies, Inc.

Copyright © 2012 Sue Stockdale and Clive Steeper

The moral rights of the author have been asserted

Database right Hodder Education (makers)

The *Teach Yourself* name is a registered trademark of Hachette UK.

British Library Cataloguing in Publication Data: a catalogue record for this
title is available from the British Library.

Library of Congress Catalog Card Number: on file.

10 9 8 7 6 5 4 3 2 1

The publisher has used its best endeavours to ensure that any website
addresses referred to in this book are correct and active at the time of going
to press. However, the publisher and the author have no responsibility for
the websites and can make no guarantee that a site will remain live or that
the content will remain relevant, decent or appropriate.

The publisher has made every effort to mark as such all words which it
believes to be trademarks. The publisher should also like to make it clear
that the presence of a word in the book, whether marked or unmarked, in
no way affects its legal status as a trademark.

Every reasonable effort has been made by the publisher to trace the
copyright holders of material in this book. Any errors or omissions should
be notified in writing to the publisher, who will endeavour to rectify the
situation for any reprints and future editions.

Hachette UK's policy is to use papers that are natural, renewable and
recyclable products and made from wood grown in sustainable forests.
The logging and manufacturing processes are expected to conform to the
environmental regulations of the country of origin.

www.hoddereducation.co.uk

Cover image © 2happy – Fotolia

Typeset by Cenveo Publisher Services.

Printed in Great Britain by CPI Group (UK) Ltd, Croydon, CR0 4YY.

Acknowledgements

Thanks to those we have worked with over the years who have provided such useful learning opportunities on how to cope with change and bounce back from disappointment. Your experiences have provided the basis for us to write this book.

To our readers – remember it's never too late to change.

Contents

1

Introduction

In this chapter you will learn:

- *About change from the worker's point of view*
- *About the importance of managing change well*
- *About stress and wellbeing*

Everyone thinks of changing the world, but no one thinks of changing himself.

Leo Tolstoy

One of the situations that most of us face on a regular basis at work is coping with change. There are many books that exist to help managers deal with this issue, in order to create strategies to get 'buy in' and commitment from their employees. However, there are fewer books that focus on the issue from the perspective of the 'worker' i.e. the one who is experiencing the change being done 'to them'. Very often in this situation, employees can feel helpless, as they perceive they have little choice but to go along with what is happening because someone much higher up the pecking order is orchestrating the changes.

This book turns its attention to this issue so that workers do not have to feel they are helpless with few choices, but instead have the resources to be able to cope and adapt. Furthermore, by reviewing actions taken and learning some coping techniques, they can be prepared and ready to anticipate future situations at work where individuals are required to undertake some type of change. After all, the reality is that in life, the *only person you can change is yourself.*

As you read through this book, there are likely to be a number of questions that come to your mind, in order for you to evaluate if it will be of benefit to you. If you read the questions and answers below they will help you decide if the book can help you to address the type of changes you may face at work now and in the future.

Self-assessment

1 What will this book give you?

2 What type of changes are you currently facing at work?

3 How have you coped with change before?

4 How does this book help you to learn about change?

5 Is this about business change or life change?

6 Is this book just for managers?

7 How does this book help you to understand how change impacts on others?

8 Will this book help you manage the interface between work and life?

9 How can this book help you to anticipate change in future?

10 You have limited time – will you have to read it from cover to cover to learn the key concepts?

Answers

1 This book will give you practical advice and ideas on how to cope with change at work. Through a number of work-based scenarios, the book explains the change process in each situation from the perspective of the change being 'done to you'.

2 Different change situations will raise different issues for you as an employee. Each chapter highlights a particular work-based situation you may encounter: from redundancy and getting a new job, to change caused by others, or management-imposed changes, as well as the introduction of new systems and procedures and what happens when teams merge in an organization.

3 Think back to changes that you have experienced at work so far in your career. How did you deal with them? Maybe some you coped with successfully and others caused you to feel resistant, uncertain or anxious. You will learn practical tips to deal with a variety of situations which will help you to be more prepared and anticipate what may happen if you encounter these situations in the future.

4 It helps you learn about change by framing each chapter around a simple four-stage model of change, so that there is consistency between one section and another which makes it easier for you to cross refer.

5 This book mainly discusses coping with change at work. However, there is one chapter that relates the learning from work to coping with change in your personal life too. Also many of the techniques discussed will be relevant in a wider context than purely a work setting.

6 This book will be ideal for workers, particularly at junior and mid level, as well as first line managers or others who find themselves having to cope with change, rather than being responsible for implementing it.

7 One of the key points about coping with change is being able to step into the shoes of others and have some empathy and understanding. In the chapter scenarios, there are questions and ideas to help you consider the situation from a wider perspective.

8 Often when people find themselves under pressure at work due to changes being undertaken in the organization, it can spill into their personal lives when they find it difficult to 'switch off' and relax, and they become irritable and short tempered. The book provides methods of coping so that you can leave the stresses of work behind when you go home and get on with your life in a more relaxed manner.

9 By reviewing situations that you have experienced and learning new behaviours, you will be able to not only cope with existing change, but get prepared for likely future scenarios too.

10 The structure of the book enables you to read each chapter as a stand-alone guide to the particular situation that it refers to; you won't necessarily have to read through the entire book.

There are plenty of examples of workers who have to cope with a myriad of changes these days. Take the experience of two brothers, James and Bryan, who had both finished their education and entered the world of employment. James had studied tourism at university for three years, before getting a job in a global travel firm based in London. Bryan, on the other hand, was not sure what direction his career should take and had been working in a public sector organization since leaving university.

During the Christmas holidays they caught up over a beer at home. James commented that his year at work had been particularly hectic. The travel company had been taken over by a competitor, which meant his office had merged with another. It had been chaotic whilst the management decided which jobs were to remain and which ones made redundant. In the end James kept his job, but had to learn how to use a new computer system and was now working from a different office location in London, which gave him an extra 45-minute commute from home. And now the culture seemed far more about making profit and achieving targets than delivering any form of customer service.

Whilst Bryan empathized, he also had experienced his fair share of change. With the economic downturn, the public sector organization had made major cutbacks, and 8 per cent of the workforce had been made redundant. Bryan was one of the youngest employees, so was lucky that his specialist knowledge of a particular type of technology had enabled him to keep his job.

However, there was pretty low morale in the office. Even at meetings, no one was given free tea and coffee any more, not even when external clients visited, and every cost was monitored closely. His manager had taken to checking his work to a minute level of detail and constantly changing the objectives, which was driving Bryan mad. If he complained, he was told that he was 'lucky to have a job at all' and should stop moaning. It appeared that both had experienced a number of changes in their organizations, and were not entirely sure that they had coped very well.

Remember this

Everyone experiences change at work and people often develop short term ways of coping with it. When you begin to feel that you have no control of the situation, or are entering the unknown, this can increase your stress levels and therefore potentially affect your ability to perform well at work. Knowing how to cope with change will help you to reduce stress, feel more in control and be able to perform more effectively at work.

The essence of this book lies in the concepts, tools and examples, which will help you to navigate through changes that you may be facing now or will face in the future. They may also help you to understand previous changes you've experienced and then be able to put them into a better perspective.

Chapter 2 outlines what happens during change and introduces the four-stage change process that is used in every subsequent chapter. Chapter 3 describes some change management successes and demonstrates the application of the behaviours used to cope with change.

Chapters 4 to 12 tackle different workplace change scenarios and provide ideas and techniques to help you to manage in those situations. These scenarios are: change caused by others, external changes forced on an organization, management-imposed change, merging teams, new systems and procedures, redundancy, starting a new job, job challenges and too many changes all at once.

Chapter 13 is focused on the future, and enables you to use the learning from previous chapters in order to be ready to anticipate future change. Chapter 14 takes the change concepts and demonstrates how they can be also applied to broader life situations.

Key Idea

Typically a SWOT analysis is used to identify strengths, weaknesses, opportunities and threats to an organization. Then a plan is created to minimize areas of weakness and limit threats, whilst maximizing opportunities and strengths.

Figure 1.1 highlights which chapters in the book tackle situations that are, on the whole, internally or externally driven. For example, it is likely to be your personal choice to start a new job, whereas being made redundant is something that *happens to you* and therefore externally driven. It is likely to be a matter of your personal perspective as to whether you agree that the situations identified as 'externally driven' are either opportunities or threats!

▶ **Internal Factors – where the individual is in control**

Strengths – Chapters 9, 13 and 14 (Starting a new job; Anticipating change and Applying change principles in life) generally focus on maximizing personal strengths and ideas on how to be proactive to achieve what you want.

Weaknesses – Chapters 11 and 12 (Job challenges and Too many changes all at once) explore stressful situations at work that may highlight weaknesses which should be addressed or minimized.

▶ **External Factors – mainly instigated by others**

Opportunities – Chapters 7, 8 and 10 (Merging teams; New systems and procedures and Redundancy) explain how changes brought about by external factors can create opportunities for development to be maximized.

Threats – Chapters 4, 5 and 6 (Change caused by others; External changes on organization and Management-imposed change) highlight external situations that can appear threatening when there is an element of unknown. By minimizing the risks and gaining more certainty, this can turn threats into opportunities.

	Strengths	Weaknesses
Internal Factors	Chapter 9 Starting a New Job Chapter 13 Anticipating Change Chapter 14 Applying Change Principles in Life	Chapter 11 Job Challenges Chapter 12 Too many changes all at once
	Opportunities	**Threats**
External Factors	Chapter 7 Merging Teams Chapter 8 New Systems and Procedures Chapter 10 Redundancy	Chapter 4 Change Caused by Others Chapter 5 External Changes on Organisation Chapter 6 Management Imposed Change

Figure 1.1 Internal and external factors

Try it now

Use this book to create your own change navigation tool kit. As you read through each chapter, keep notes and think about things that you could do to help you take control, minimize the unknown factors and move through the change process more quickly.

Being able to cope with change at work effectively is not just another activity to add to the 'to do' list because if people are unable to change, it costs their organization, and the UK as a whole, a lot of money. According to Health and Safety Executive (HSE) reports, in 2005/6 work-related stress, depression and anxiety cost the UK in excess of £530 million. The number of workers who had sought medical advice for what they believed to be work-related stress increased by 110,000 to an estimated 530,000.

The HSE has created some good practice 'Stress Management Standards' which are designed to address areas that, if not managed well, can lead to health and productivity issues at work. The five areas are:

▶ Change – e.g. how change is managed and communicated in an organization

▶ Demands – e.g. workload, work patterns and the work environment

▶ Control – e.g. how much say the person has in the way they do their work

▶ Support – e.g. encouragement and resources provided by the organization

▶ Role – e.g. the degree of clarity that people have about their role within the organization

Remember this

The inability to cope with change can impact on health, productivity, well being and motivation at work. Figure 1.2 illustrates how performance is affected. As individual stress or arousal increases from low to medium, performance increases. If this continues from medium to high, performance then decreases.

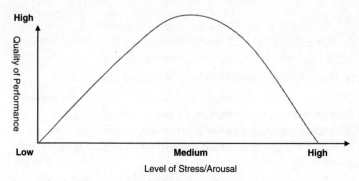

Task Performance Curve

Quality of Performance — High / Low

Level of Stress/Arousal — Low / Medium / High

Figure 1.2 The effects of stress on performance at work

Each person will have their own definition of what is low, medium and high stress. In times of change if the level of stress is too low, an individual may react rather than anticipate what action is required to be taken. However at the other end of the curve, when there is high stress individuals:

▶ may get tunnel vision and only focus on a narrow view of the situation

▶ use past experience to behave in a similar manner regardless of whether that behaviour is appropriate

▶ don't want to discuss options or alternatives but become fixed in their thinking.

There is an optimal amount of stress that everyone requires to perform effectively, and being able to manage stress effectively is an important factor.

According to the US Coast Guard (http://www.uscg.mil), when people face high stress situations, they can adopt five hazardous thinking patterns that have a major effect on their ability to adapt to a changing situation. The thought patterns are:

▶ Anti-authority

▶ Impulsiveness

- Invincibility
- Macho
- Resignation

▶ Pattern 1: Anti-authority *'no one tells me what to do'*

People at work who resent being told what to do or 'controlled' in a change situation are likely to behave in a way that is different even from their own better judgement. This is purely because they just don't want to do what an authority figure tells them to do.

Solution: If this is a pattern you use, or recognize, remember that there are always policies, procedures and rules in organizations that you will be held accountable to.

▶ Pattern 2: Impulsiveness *'do something, now – anything'*

This is behaviour under stress where a person feels they have to just take any action, without thinking through what the implications may be.

Solution: Stop, take a breath, and think. Slowing down and noticing breathing will give your brain the chance to catch up and not go into automatic action.

▶ Pattern 3: Invincibility – *'It will never happen to me'*

This pattern shows when someone is in denial and believes that any change situation will never impact on them. It is not about their overestimated capabilities but a lack of awareness of the implications of the change about to happen.

Solution: Think about previous change experiences and review what ACTUALLY happened to get a better view of reality.

▶ Pattern 4: Macho – *'I can do it'*

This pattern is about those that want to prove they are better than others and are driven to step out of their comfort zone as a result. They often take unnecessary risks, and overestimate their own capabilities.

Solution: There is not always a need to prove your brilliance to others, and put yourself and maybe other colleagues into risky situations. Become aware of what is really driving you and accept that others are likely to already be aware of your capabilities.

▶ **Pattern 5: Resignation –** *'What's the point?'*

In a stressful situation, a person who adopts this thinking pattern does not believe that their contribution will be of value, so prefer to take no action and wait for others to do something. They don't want to take responsibility.

Solution: Ask yourself the question, 'what difference could I make here?' and begin to notice that even a small action could help and bring a different perspective to a change situation.

Try it now

Review your thinking patterns and observe if you tend to adopt any of the five hazardous thinking patterns when you encounter a high stress situation. Consider a different type of behaviour that you could adopt the next time it happens.

Next steps

The upcoming chapter will take you through the change process in detail, which will be referred to in each subsequent chapter. This process will be the framework to help increase understanding.

2

What happens during change?

In this chapter you will learn:

- ► *About the framework for change*
- ► *About the change curve and the four phases of change*

Self-assessment

Think of your current work situation and answer the following questions:

1 Which aspects of work do you think may require some change?

2 What has stopped you addressing them so far?

3 What is likely to change?

4 How urgent is the change?

5 Who is likely to be involved?

6 How does it affect you?

7 What might cause resistance?

8 What will success look like?

9 How do you expect to make the changes that are needed?

10 How will you measure and pace progress?

Answers

1 It is important for you to take a wider view of issues at work that may have an impact on your job. Often people get caught up focusing on their particular area and miss or ignore a major change that is going on elsewhere in the business which may have implications for them and their team.

2 Understanding resistance helps to pinpoint where the real issues are that need to be tackled in any change situation.

3 This helps to translate a broad description into a greater level of detail. For example, if the business is moving to a new location, this question helps you to think about issues like travel time, parking, type of office etc.

4 Putting boundary limits or levels of priority on a likely change helps to identify what actions may need to be taken immediately and those that can be phased in at a later stage. This enables you to focus on the critical issues knowing that others are being monitored to ensure they are within the set boundary.

5 Resistance to change can be caused by others not getting involved at an early enough stage in decisions, or not being given clear communication about how the change will affect them. Consider who is likely to be needed in discussing the change, and who will be impacted by the change. Then create a plan to get them involved as soon as possible.

6 Make sure you understand how any changes will affect you personally because if you are not committed to a change, it is extremely difficult to inspire others to be committed to it.

7 Think ahead to what might be the areas of resistance from others. By 'stepping into their shoes' you can view the issue from a different perspective. Avoid delegating if you have limited enthusiasm or interest, as resistance can be caused when the recipient of a task senses that they are being 'dumped upon'.

8 By creating a vision of what the successful change will result in, can help you get committed and also be convincing to others when explaining what is going on. For example, you might imagine what you will see, hear and feel like when you are inside the new office. Then you can describe it to others and you know what you are aiming for as a result of making the changes.

9 Create an action plan with timescales. By taking action during change helps to keep others on board and enables you to maintain momentum. The most frustrating situations can be when people know a change is about to happen, but nothing is actually happening. The feeling of being in suspended animation can cause a lot of stress for those involved.

10 By measuring progress and pace against your plan, it gives you a sense of taking action, it can be communicated to others and can increase motivation and commitment from others as they see the change taking shape. Getting acceptance, or 'buy in', from others is paramount.

This chapter will help you understand what actually happens during change. Whether it's moving to a new desk in the office or merging two teams together as part of the company restructure, the process is similar. By understanding what is going on, it can help you to cope better next time you have to either deal with a change yourself or manage others through a changing situation.

Case study

Claire managed a team of three employees who were based alongside her at the company HQ in London. Each was responsible for looking after a region of the UK, which meant a lot of travel to visit their clients in the regions. The structure had been in place for a number of years and her team had just got used to working long hours and clocking up the miles in their cars. However, the senior management decided that it would be more efficient to have 'field based staff' who would be located in the regions. Claire did not have any involvement in the decision but it meant that she had to manage the implications within her team.

She would have to amend their job descriptions and then discuss with each person if they were interested in moving out to the region. For one, whose region was the London area, it would mean no change – would they be disappointed? Claire would have to get used to working with a virtual team, and regular communication would be much more important. It took her a few days to see the benefits and begin to like the idea of a managing a field based team.

Claire then thought about each person and how they were likely to react. She considered what would motivate them to move and how the change might benefit each one. She also thought about what might cause resistance and how to overcome those issues. It was a stressful time for her. However, when she spoke to her team, Claire was surprised at their reactions. Two of them were pleased to move out of London as it meant lower living costs and being closer to their families, and the other decided it was a good time to leave and study for a postgraduate qualification. That left Claire with the task of recruiting a new team member. She was pleased with the outcome and put in place a plan of regular conference calls and quarterly team meetings to make sure the team communicated together.

This story illustrates how important it was for the manager to be committed to the change and to think through the implications prior to communicating with her team. How often have you been told about a change by someone and you know from the way they speak and their body language that they do not believe in it themselves? It is so much harder to want to conform and agree to something when you know the leader themselves is not behind it.

Remember this

As a manager it is vital that *you* are committed to the change before you try to convince others to follow you. If it's really something you don't agree with then reflect on what *specifically* you are resisting, and ask yourself what would need to happen to make you committed to the change. Your actions will always speak louder than your words.

So whether it's the manager or an individual, everyone will experience the same process whilst undergoing change. Some will react quicker than others but everyone will experience it.

The best-known framework for change is the 'five stages of grief' cycle, pioneered in 1969 by Elisabeth Kübler-Ross in the support and counselling of personal trauma, grief and grieving, associated with death and dying. Her ideas (denial, anger, bargaining, depression and acceptance) are also relevant to personal change and conflict resolution.

This model has been adapted for this book to simplify it and make it more relevant for business. The undulations in the *change curve* denote what happens to your level of motivation during change.

Key idea

There are four stages on the change curve: Denial, Resistance, Acceptance and Commitment. Typical words and feelings you may hear and experience as you negotiate these stages are shown in Figure 2.1.

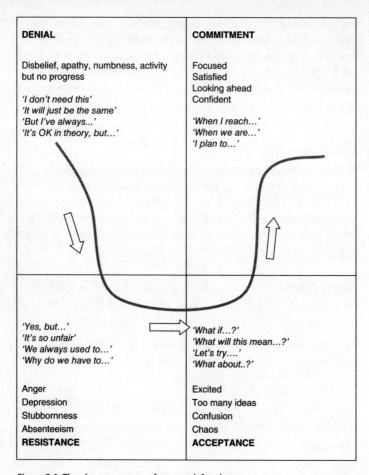

DENIAL	COMMITMENT
Disbelief, apathy, numbness, activity but no progress	Focused Satisfied Looking ahead Confident
'I don't need this' *'It will just be the same'* *'But I've always...'* *'It's OK in theory, but...'*	*'When I reach...'* *'When we are...'* *'I plan to...'*
'Yes, but...' *'It's so unfair'* *'We always used to...'* *'Why do we have to...'*	*'What if...?'* *'What will this mean...?'* *'Let's try....'* *'What about..?'*
Anger Depression Stubbornness Absenteeism **RESISTANCE**	Excited Too many ideas Confusion Chaos **ACCEPTANCE**

Figure 2.1 The change curve – a framework for change

So using this model, consider changes that you have experienced in the past. It's useful to reflect on how quickly you moved through the framework and gained commitment to the change. Or did you get stuck in resistance for a while before eventually the cajoling and encouragement of others helped you move on? Think about the impact you may have experienced when more than one change programme was going on at the same time, which is more common in large organizations these days.

So let's consider each stage in more detail as this framework will be used in each subsequent chapter to explain how to tackle specific work issues that you may encounter.

▶ Denial

What a wonderful place to be! Denial is like being on your favourite Caribbean island. As you soak up the rays whilst sprawled on the sunbed, you feel the warmth of the sun on your skin and the coolness of the breeze blowing across your body. You hear the sound of the water lapping on the shore and as you stretch across to enjoy a cool drink you just don't want to be anywhere else. Your friend sitting beside you mentions casually that they have seen a few clouds on the horizon, but you ignore them as you don't really want to think about anything spoiling your relaxation time.

When you are in denial nothing can spoil the current situation. No matter what information you hear, or signs that you may observe, you resist thinking about what the implications might be. In the world of denial, you feel safe and secure.

Look around your workplace and notice who might be currently in the land of denial. The manager who consistently refuses to listen to feedback about their behaviour, or the colleague who has been told on many occasions to tidy up their desk yet does nothing. They are focused on the present and what *is,* not on *what if* or *what might be.* They are in their 'comfort zone' and quite happy as they are and see no need to change. For the individual, there is no problem.

Case study

John had worked in the bank for 20 years. He left school at 16 and joined the business eager to build a career and develop his knowledge. Once in the organization, John realized that there were a lot of opportunities available to him. He liked working on the banking counter, getting to know the regular customers and delivering fantastic customer service. When they told him how friendly and helpful he was, it made his day. As time went by, John saw that in order to progress at work, a promotion often meant a move to a different branch, which meant more travel time and longer hours at work. And he liked what he did and did not want to move. So John decided to stay put.

As the years went by, John gained a reputation for being an outstanding clerk, and he even had managed to gain a promotion within his branch. When new employees started at work, they always spent a few days with John because he had such a good rapport with customers.

However, things were about to change in the banking environment. Pressure on costs and a drive to deliver greater profit meant that the front line retail bank's goals were changing. Service was no longer so important, and the new buzzword that replaced it was sales targets. Everything related to sales was measured and reported on and John noticed that his fellow counter staff always seemed to be trying to sell insurance or a loan to a customer when they clearly did not need it. John ignored them, and felt that if he did a good job and made the customers happy when they came in, they would continue to come in and surely that was enough? One day, shortly afterwards, John was called into the manager's office. He was asked why he was consistently falling short on sales targets and not upselling other products. His manager informed him that if he did not improve his performance he would be dismissed. It was at that moment, that John realized he had been in denial.

Denial is one of the most common defence mechanisms that everyone can use, pretending that an uncomfortable thing did not or is not happening. Often the only way to spot you are in denial is when someone else tells you. For John he saw that changes were impending but ignored them until it was almost too late.

Remember this

When in denial, you are oblivious to reality. It can be positive because it stops us being overwhelmed by multiple changes at one time. However, being in denial for too long can have disastrous consequences for both you and others. The key to change is being willing to listen and consider feedback and information from others. Be open and ask yourself *what is it that they are really trying to tell me*?

► Resistance

Resistance can be the most turbulent stage of the change process. In this phase managers are likely to experience extremes of behaviour because people can feel that they are being driven to take a particular action. For example, when a member of the team is asked to hand over a project to a colleague, their initial reaction is likely to come from the most ancient part of their brain. The primitive brain evolved millions of years ago, when humans had to hunt down their food, and its foremost trait is survival. This means the initial reaction may be to say 'no' without thinking because this change is perceived as a threat. However, once the thinking part of the brain is engaged, which enables humans to take a more considered view, there may be a different reaction.

During resistance, the focus is still on the past and what *used to be*, rather than what *could be*, so an individual will not want to think at all about the future and what it might be like once the change has occurred. In the example of giving up a project to a colleague, the team member might actually have too many projects and feel overloaded which would mean that handing one over may be the ideal solution, but depending on how it's presented, it may result in resistance.

An extreme example of resistance is when workers choose to strike in order to try to stop new work practices being introduced into their organization. Others may decide to adopt a more subtle form of resistance and suddenly have a few days off sick and make the introduction of a change more difficult to implement.

However, no matter what type of resistance is adopted, a key feature is the level of emotional energy it demands. That's why one of the words used to describe this state is depression. For some, the stress and emotional energy they use up trying to resist a change may push them towards feeling depressed and helpless.

Remember this

For most people, moving from resistance to acceptance is the most difficult transition in the change process. It takes a lot of emotional energy and stress to remain in resistance. Consider how that energy could be used more productively to accept the change and move on.

One useful technique to help people move from resistance to acceptance is to ask themselves *what if* questions. This type of question does not imply that an action needs to be taken, but helps to bridge the gap between focusing on the past and moving to the future. Imagine standing on a road looking back at the past where you have been and you have wonderful memories of all the good things that happened. You know that the road will not continue on in the same way into the future. However, asking 'what if' questions such as 'what if I don't like it?' or 'what if my team member is really great to work with?' can enable you to feel more in control and, in any change situation, people are more likely to be committed to it, if there is an element of choice and control.

Key idea

The 5 'whys' questioning method can be useful to overcome resistance and to explore the cause/effect relationships underlying a particular situation. The aim is to ultimately determine the root cause of the resistance. See the example on the next page.

I don't want to hand over the project to my colleague because it will appear I can't do my job properly.

▶ **Why?** It will take me too long to explain it to them

▶ **Why?** Because I did not write down the overall project outline

▶ **Why?** My manager has given me lots of other projects to do as well

▶ **Why?** She believes I am capable and can deliver

▶ **Why?** Because I am highly motivated and do a good job (the core belief)

So the root cause highlights that the individual wants to do a good job, and is currently not able to do so because of too many projects. Resisting the change is likely to be a self-defeating behaviour because it results in the unwanted outcome of holding on to too many projects and not delivering any on time, which in turn goes against the underlying belief.

▶ Acceptance

Many people find it difficult to *accept* change especially if it's been forced upon them with little or no consultation. Some see it as a sign of weakness that they have bowed to others' demands and not put up a fight. Yet although acceptance can seem like a hard thing to do, it is important to understand what it actually means. Many people think that if they accept a change they are agreeing with it, and that's not always the case.

For example, at a board meeting of a company the directors were discussing the possible acquisition of another business. Most of the board agreed with the proposal and felt that it would give the company additional capacity to grow internationally. Only the non-Executive Director and the Finance Director were resisting because they sensed that the investment might lead the company to overreach its financial commitments. After all the views had been aired, the Managing Director who had the majority shareholding took the decision to go ahead with the acquisition.

So, whilst the two dissenters accepted the decision it did not mean that they agreed with it, and they still felt that the Managing Director had been over optimistic. However, they did acknowledge that the MD was a risk taker, while they were more risk averse, and it would either be a great success or a dismal failure. So it's OK to disagree, and accepting a change does not mean that there is agreement with another's values or beliefs.

By contrast, some others can get enthused in the acceptance phase and by beginning to think about the new future they are excited to make it happen. Their focus is firmly in the future, and what they can do to move on. This enthusiasm and rush of ideas can bring with it a level of chaos as the new direction is not yet clearly defined.

Within one organization, when it was announced that they were going to start having monthly social activities to build better working relationships, many people came up with great ideas of events they would like to organize. Soon there was chaos with activities happening on the same day, no communication about what the purpose was and nearly all the annual budget was spent in the first three months!

All of this energy and evidence of progress is good news too, because it can help those who are still in resistance to see that the change is possible. Some people don't like to be the initiators of change, and are happy to follow along once others have paved the way and sorted out the chaos. The evidence of results motivates this type of individual to get on board too.

It is vital however, that once people have changed their focus from the past to the future, and actions are being taken, that a clearer direction is defined which enables all the resources to be harnessed more effectively towards the changed situation. That's where the final phase of commitment begins.

► Commitment

There is a sense of definiteness to the *commitment* phase. By now specific action has been defined to implement the change, people have 'bought' into it and clarity of direction has been established. It's beginning to seem like it will be a reality rather than an idea. An important activity in the commitment phase is measuring progress.

Key idea

In order to monitor the speed of change, implementing relevant measures are vital. What gets measured gets done, so make sure the measures are meaningful and communicated to everyone involved. Use them to build commitment to the plan and be prepared to review them as the actions progress towards the overall goal.

It's a great feeling when a manager has a high level of commitment to make a change happen. Everyone is involved in working towards a common vision, and understands why the change is happening, regular feedback on progress is provided and commitment is high.

Commitment brings a sense of empowerment to individuals. Think about how you behave when you are committed to something. People will go the extra mile, work longer hours just to complete the task because they know that it will make a difference. It's not an accident that when annual surveys like the *Sunday Times* '100 Best Companies to Work For' are published there is a high correlation between the commitment and engagement of employees and retention levels within the companies.

The change process is not a one way journey however. People can move back down the curve depending on their experience. If they are one of the first to commit to a change and then it's slow to materialize or others don't buy in, they may find themselves questioning if it's really the right thing to do. Having support and encouragement from others and open and honest communication will help to maintain a level of commitment to change.

Focus points

Everyone experiences going through the change curve many times in their work lives, what will vary from person to person is how quickly they navigate the change.

There are four phases of change: Denial, Resistance, Acceptance and Commitment.

Viewing any change from another's perspective can bring new insight. If there is resistance – find out what's really stopping the individual from moving forwards.

Denial and *resistance* phases are past focused; *acceptance* and *commitment* phases are future focused.

Next steps

The next chapter will explain how people at work have applied the knowledge of this change curve to navigate change successfully. The subsequent chapters will focus on typical change scenarios that people are likely to experience at work and how to address them specifically so that they will be prepared to tackle them effectively in future.

Navigating change successfully

In this chapter you will learn:

- ► *About successful change navigation*
- ► *How to assess your behaviour*
- ► *What helps you move round the change curve*

Self-assessment

Think of your current work situation and answer the following questions:

1. What changes at work can you think of that you have navigated successfully?

2. What did you do that worked well?

3. What was the outcome as a result of your coping well?

4. What did not go well?

5. What surprised you and why?

6. What impact did your behaviour have on others around you, and vice versa?

7. What facets of your personality would you say affect your ability to navigate change successfully?

8. If you had a blind spot about change, what would it be?

9. What are the parameters of the changes that you are currently facing?

10. With hindsight, what improvements would you make to ensure that you can navigate change successfully in future?

Answers

1. It is always useful to think about successes and what worked because sometimes people tend to focus on the negative and changes that did not work as planned. It is also likely that the changes that went smoothly and caused you no hassle were not so memorable emotionally, hence the importance of reviewing them here and getting a more balanced viewpoint.

2. By focusing specifically on the behaviours that you demonstrated, you can create a stronger mental image of what to do when you face a change situation. It may be that you quickly moved round the change curve to become committed, because you were focused on the future benefits, listened to others and formed your own opinion rather than being swayed by office rumour. Or it may be that the outcome was going to

make your life at work better, so you were keen to get involved in the change.

3 Attitude drives behaviour and behaviour drives outcome, so your response to question 2 will help you move to the next step (review the outcome that you got as a result).

4 There may be some elements of the change that did not go so well, maybe because they were unexpected and you had not thought about them which created uncertainty or a feeling of lack of control. Being honest with yourself will help you to gain a true perspective of what worked and what did not work so that you can do things differently next time.

5 A surprising outcome may happen as a result of how you behave in a change situation, as often you have fixed expectations about how others will behave. For example, if your mindset was '*if my colleague asks me to work late because there is a late change to the monthly report, I shall just say no*' and then on the day, when she asked you to help her, you agreed. A surprising outcome may be that your boss speaks to you and thanks you for being a team player and helping your colleague.

6 Noticing the wider impact is a useful exercise because a small action can have a significant change on someone else. Think about your boss, peers, colleagues in other departments, and people outside work that may have been affected by your actions.

7 Knowing yourself well will help you predict how you are likely to manage change. In this chapter, you will learn about a personality profiling tool called Myers-Briggs Type Indicator® (MBTI), which highlights the different behaviour preferences that people can demonstrate. For example, if you have a preference for detail over the big picture, you may be reluctant to accept a change until you have understood it in detail.

8 It is impossible to see ourselves as others see us, and sometimes you will have a blind spot to how your behaviour is perceived or the impact it has on others. One way to begin to reveal our blind spots is to solicit feedback from others. The Johari Window model will explain this later in this chapter.

9 You need to know the limitations of the change situation you may be facing in order to know what options you have for action. For example, if you were a police officer, one parameter that is relevant for you would be operating within the law, whereas an office administrator may have speed and accuracy as the key parameters that will impact on the success of their change issue.

10 Having reviewed your experience to date, decide if you coped the way you wanted to in the changes you dealt with. If so, write down the key lessons for you about change; if not, think about what you need to alter to be better placed to deal with change the next time round. This chapter will give you examples of successful change situations so that you can build up some tips and techniques for yourself that will be helpful in future.

Remember this

Yesterday's behaviours are not the sole predictors of the likelihood of success tomorrow. Whilst you may have managed with the implementation of a new system or procedures, which only marginally affected you personally, it may not be entirely the same as being made redundant or changing jobs. Think about the key principles that may apply in general situations but always think specifically about the nuances of each change situation you encounter, as they will all be different.

Whilst the world of business has many examples of successful changes being implemented, there are also many examples from outside work that can draw out the same lessons and metaphors. One of these situations occurs in the Arctic environment, where those who attempt to travel in the freezing temperatures face constant changes because of the extreme weather, which of course they cannot control.

Take the experience of a team of four adventurers who in 1999 attempted to ski across the Greenland Ice Cap, a distance of over 350 miles. They would be hauling sledges weighing over 60 kg each, containing all the food, fuel and equipment that they would need to survive.

They started out on the first day of the expedition with lots of enthusiasm and motivation, which very nearly dissipated due to unforeseen changes. The unseasonably warm temperatures meant the ice had melted in places, which forced the team to make a detour. The rough terrain on this alternative route caused the shaft on one of the sledges to break. Luckily one of the Norwegians in the team was able to fix the problem using various bits of equipment he had, and this enabled them to continue.

Then a few days later another of the team members developed a muscle strain in his leg which was extremely painful. It meant that some of the equipment in his sledge had to be re-allocated to others in order to lighten his load and make pulling the sledge more bearable. The others in the team were committed to this because they understood the reason for the change and knew that if they were to stand a chance of being successful, it would mean a little extra hardship for them all.

Just as the team thought they were making progress, another external factor threatened their success. There was a fierce storm that lasted for two days, which meant temperatures plummeted due to wind chill, and ice crystals were being blown around, making it impossible to travel. Rather than get downhearted, or give up entirely, the team members discussed the options that were available to them and reviewed their original goal to see if it was still feasible.

Every day when they were tent bound, meant another day of eating into their rations, which were carefully planned for a finite number of days. So they decided to forego eating much, to conserve the food for the remainder of the expedition. Inside the tent, spirits waned as each team member faced up to the possibility of failure.

Eventually the wind died down and they were able to continue their journey, eventually completing the crossing in 28 days. They had been so conservative with their food and fuel that they ended up with three days extra supply when they finished!

Remember this

When external factors impact on you at work and cause a change situation, one way to think about it is that potentially everyone in the organization may be suffering from the same hardship. As long as the team was originally committed to achieving the goal, and the goal still remains clearly defined, external threats can sometimes galvanize a team to really pull together to overcome the threat.

Sometimes you can be unaware of the positive impact that your behaviour during a change has on others, and once you receive that feedback, it can keep you motivated and make you feel good about yourself.

The Johari Window (devised by Joseph Luft and Harry Ingham) in Figure 3.1 explains how feedback and self disclosure are two activities that can help you discover more about your unknown potential. The Arena is the public arena in which you generally operate and is known to you and others. The areas of the Blind Spot and Façade contain elements of your behaviour that are either unknown to you or unknown to others.

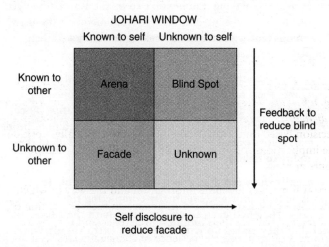

Figure 3.1 The Johari Window

Try it now

Taking some time to reflect about change situations that you have experienced and asking others for their views about your behaviour, can help you reduce blind spots and enable you to reveal something more of yourself to others.

Another tool that can help you to learn more about yourself is the Myers-Briggs Type Indicator® (MBTI). This is a psychometric questionnaire designed to measure preferences in how people perceive the world and make decisions. There are four dichotomies, two of which are based on the psychological types that Carl Jung identified below:

▶ The 'rational' (judging) functions: *thinking* and *feeling*

▶ The 'irrational' (perceiving) functions: *sensing* and *intuition*

For example, some people have a preference for *sensing* and noticing lots of detail, whereas others will prefer *intuition* and use their so-called 'sixth sense' to make connections and see future possibilities as they take in information. If two people are told about a new system to be implemented in their department, here's what might happen.

Person A has a sensing and thinking preference.

Person B has an intuition and feeling preference.

Person A uses their *sensing function* to ask specific questions e.g. *when are the systems to be implemented? What information is available?* Having taken in the responses, Person A makes a decision based on their *thinking* function to rationally work out the implications for themselves and if it will require additional hours at work.

Person B receives the same information and the way in which it is delivered is likely to have an impact on their perception of it. Person B will use their *intuition* preference and may make a connection to another experience of change which was not implemented effectively. With their feeling preference, which can generate interest in maintaining harmony they might ask a question about *how is it likely to impact the people in the team?*

When the change actually happens, Person A may be an ideal person to check all the details prior to implementation, whilst Person B could think about how the messages should be communicated to the team in order to have the best chance of a positive outcome. The point is that once you know what your preferences are and how you are likely to behave, you can learn how to manage yourself and also appreciate the differences in others who behave differently from you.

Key idea

Understanding personality preferences helps you appreciate and value difference, and since the only person you can change is yourself, it's about developing ways to adapt your behaviour to get on better with others.

WHAT HELPS YOU TO MOVE ROUND THE CHANGE CURVE?

As discussed in Chapter 2, the four stages that people typically experience during change are denial, resistance, acceptance and commitment. By considering where one's focus is, it can help to provide more detail about the specific actions that can help you to move through the process speedily.

Typically, in denial and resistance, people are focused on the past and want things to remain as they were. Then there is a move to focus on the present in both Resistance and Acceptance which then moves you into the future and commitment (and hopefully not backwards into resistance).

A template has been created on the following pages which provides a checklist of items to consider or questions to ask yourself that can take you through the change curve in any situation. Refer back to this template when you read subsequent chapters of the book.

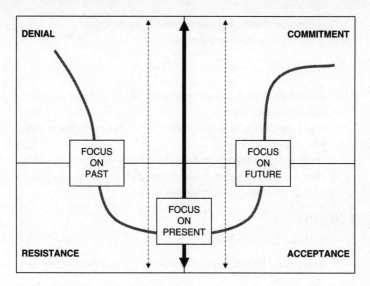

Figure 3.2 Moving round the change curve

▶ FOCUS ON PAST

Review existing experience

- ✓ Think about change situations you have already encountered
- ✓ What were the reasons behind the change?
- ✓ What did you learn from that experience?
- ✓ What enabled you to move from denial through resistance and acceptance to commitment?

▶ FOCUS ON PRESENT

Reality

- ✓ What is the current change that you are facing?
- ✓ Is it internal or external (see Chapter 1)?
- ✓ Are you committed to it, or currently resisting?
- ✓ If resisting, what is it you are actually resisting?

Gain a wider perspective

- ✓ Assess the wider landscape of the change
- ✓ Ask your manager for more information

✓ What type of risks might be involved in the change?
✓ Who else is involved or impacted?

Identify personal behaviours

✓ Remind yourself of your personality preference and how you typically like to behave
✓ If you were to step into the shoes of others involved, what is their perspective?
✓ What could you learn from them?
✓ How are you going to measure progress?
✓ Notice and manage your emotions

▶ FUTURE

Consider the possibilities

✓ What would have to happen in order for you to be committed to the change?
✓ What elements of this can you influence?

Develop a future focus

✓ Create a plan to deal with change differently in future
✓ Look for trends to indicate if another change may be imminent
✓ What is the first thing you will notice that will be different?
✓ Develop a strategy to cope with the difficult and uncomfortable
✓ What needs to be in place to ensure you remain committed to the change?

Try it now

Use the questions in the template to work through a change-related issue that you are currently facing at work. See what new insight you get and ask yourself – where is your focus now in relation to this change? Denial, resistance, acceptance or commitment?

The story of Frederick below highlights the issue of knowing where your focus is, which can help you to navigate the change curve quickly.

Case study

Frederick worked in a small, not for profit organization and was responsible for delivering various projects. He was hard working, conscientious and generally well-liked by others. Normally he had no trouble getting the board to agree to the proposals he put forward to achieve project outcomes.

However, a new board member was appointed who was known for being challenging and argumentative, and focusing on his own agenda. When Frederick put forward the next proposal to the board, he found himself being questioned and challenged by this board member. Rather than taking a moment to listen and think about what was being asked, Frederick reacted badly, raised his voice and argued back, creating an uncomfortable situation for everyone at the meeting.

As a result, the proposals were not agreed and Frederick was told to come up with some other ideas. He was incensed and thought that the board member was just being difficult for no good reason. At every meeting from then on Frederick found that the board member would challenge his ideas – it was like the behaviour of two animals vying to see who would be 'top dog'. It consumed a lot of Frederick's nervous energy and his stress levels increased because he was stuck in resistance and unwilling to accept this other person's perspective.

Frederick realized he had to change and so went for a coffee with his friend, John, to talk about the situation. John asked him to think about the situation from the board member's perspective. He also suggested that by doing this, Frederick did not have to agree with the point of view, just accept that it may be different. John also asked him to think about what he was really resisting and in what way were both the board member and Frederick's personalities different?

Once Frederick stopped and thought about these points, he realized that he had to change. Why use all that energy to get stressed when it could be used productively to make a difference on other projects?

At the next meeting, when the board member questioned him about the proposals, Frederick stopped, took a deep breath and asked him a question in order to understand the reason for the challenge. He listened and then asked further questions. As a result, the board member found himself changing his view and not being so dogmatic, and a compromise was reached.

Key idea

Frederick's behaviour illustrates the key points in the change template which helped him move from present to a future focus, and thus stop resisting. He then gained acceptance and commitment to change by considering reality, gaining a wider perspective and understanding his behaviours. Frederick also reflected that by taking time to think about the situation he could choose a different approach.

Often when you are resistant to change, it is useful to assess the situation from a number of different perspectives which can help you move through the change curve. John Grinder and Judith DeLozier (two well-known experts in Neurolinguistic programming) refer to these perspectives as perceptual positions. This exercise gives you a balanced approach to thinking about an event or outcome.

The three perceptual positions are:

▶ **First position:** considering the situation through your own eyes, ears and feelings. You think in terms of what is important to **you**, what **you** want to achieve.

▶ **Second position:** stepping into the shoes of the other person and experiencing (seeing, hearing and feeling) the situation as if you were them.

▶ **Third position:** standing back from a situation and experiencing it as if you were a detached observer. It's a bit like having a bird's eye perspective where you notice the interaction between you and the other person and consider what advice would be offered as someone who is not involved. You need to be in a relaxed state, to take an objective view of your own behaviour and look for ways to respond differently in order to achieve a different and more positive outcome.

Try it now

Sit in your chair to consider the issue from your perspective, and then move to another chair to experience it from the other person's viewpoint.

> Finally stand behind the chairs and take on the detached observer role. From this position, offer advice to yourself about how you could behave differently.

The process of navigating change successfully relies on you taking control of your own behaviour. Understanding the four stages of the process, and taking time out to consider where you are on the change curve in relation to any change that you may encounter, will help you to come up with ideas to allow you move forwards.

Stage of change curve	Characteristics of stage	What helps you move on?
Denial	When someone is in denial, they refuse to acknowledge a stressful problem or situation, avoid facing the facts of the situation and minimize the consequences. Being in denial gives your mind the opportunity to unconsciously absorb distressing information at a pace that does not cause unwanted psychological consequences.	If there is a likelihood of the situation getting worse if you do nothing, then: ▶ Honestly ask yourself what you fear. ▶ Think about the potential negative consequences of not taking action. ▶ Allow yourself to express your fears and emotions. ▶ Try to identify irrational beliefs about your situation. ▶ Open up to a trusted friend or loved one.
Resistance	People tend to resist when: ▶ The reason for the change is unclear. ▶ The change threatens to modify established working relationships between people. ▶ People have not been consulted about the change, and it is offered to them as fait accompli. ▶ There is insufficient communication about the change. ▶ The benefits and rewards for making the change are not seen as adequate for the effort required. ▶ The change threatens jobs, power or status in the organization.	Think about the wider perspective so that you can get a more balanced view of the pros and cons. Ask yourself what is it you are actually resisting? Find out more information from those who have it. Think about the benefits to you in the longer term. Consider who can support you in taking the steps required. See if there is a way to test the waters without making a full commitment to the change.

Stage of change curve	Characteristics of stage	What helps you move on?
Accept-ance	Acceptance occurs when: ▷ An individual can quickly come to terms with reality. ▷ The emotions around the change have faded sufficiently to not cloud judgement.	Recognize that it's really about you and not other people. Find people to support you. Acknowledge that you have already gone through denial and acceptance. Be clear about the difference between rumours and reality so that you can accept reality. Take responsibility for yourself.
Commit-ment	Commitment occurs when there is enthusiasm for the change and a deter-mination to work hard at it.	Be aware that there are two elements to being committed: at an intellectual level and at an emotional level. They may not necessarily happen concurrently. Building lasting commitment takes time, so don't try to short-cut the process. Be clear about how commitment is defined and measured. What actually is different? Use the plan and review process, as Frederick did in the case study.

Remember, if you stay in denial and resistance for a period of time, there will be a short term pay-off to you because you can stay in your comfort zone. However, it is likely to use up energy and introduce stress that could be put to better use in providing the impetus for getting up the curve on the other side.

The more changes that you experience, the greater the knowledge you will have about strategies to cope with and anticipate change in the future. It can be as simple as driving to work using a different route occasionally, or putting on your socks in a different order, or sitting in a different chair in your living room in the evening. Get used to change and you will be better placed to deal with it effectively.

Focus points

Focus on the past by reviewing existing experience and what you have learned already about change.

Focus on the present by considering reality, gaining a wider perspective of a situation and identifying personal behaviours. You could try a profiling tool like MBTI to assess your preferences.

Focus on the future by considering what the benefits of change will be and who can help you to remain committed.

Next steps

The next chapter examines the aspect of change caused by others. In particular, it looks at moving from a position of resistance to acceptance, and the role that curiosity can play in this process.

4

Change caused by others

In this chapter you will learn:

- ▶ *How to use rewards and respites*
- ▶ *About relationship boundaries*
- ▶ *About moving from resistance to acceptance*

Self-assessment

Think of your current work situation and answer the following questions:

1 What caused the change you are experiencing?

2 How did you react to the change?

3 What is the purpose of the change?

4 What other effects will the change have on the world around you?

5 What is your role in the change?

6 How does the change affect you?

7 What aspects of the change would you like to be done differently?

8 What aspects of the change might challenge you?

9 Who is in your support team for the change?

10 How will you keep yourself 'on track' with the change?

Answers

1 When faced with changes that come from outside your everyday world it is important to make the time to understand how the change (i) relates to the business and (ii) impacts the other things you do.

2 There is a discussion of denial in each chapter of the book so by now you'll probably recognize that when a change happens to you, it is important to ensure your feelings about it are genuine and founded on substance rather than the often natural inclination to simply reject new changes, especially if they are a surprise! Bearing in mind how significant first impressions can be, if the change is coming from outside your 'normal' world, and from someone new to you, it may be especially important to act how you want to be perceived and not just how you feel.

3 If you can understand the reason for the change then it means your decisions and approach can be more balanced and effective. Also, people from outside your day-to-day job may not appreciate your perspective so may (i) assume you understand the significance and relevance of their change (to the business) and (ii) not fully understand your role and priorities. Therefore it is very important to ensure that both parties understand each other's expectations and constraints.

4 It can be a very worthwhile first step to make sure you understand the importance and impact of change from both sides, i.e. consider it from both your perspective and that of those responsible for instigating the change. The change may seem incremental to others but actually be a significant 'step' change to you and your team or vice versa. Either way if all parties are not aligned then there is a very real potential for conflict or, worse still, failure to fully deliver the change.

5 Following on from question 4, being clear about your role and associated expectations is vital. All too often assumptions are made about what people's roles, authorities, areas of responsibilities and expectations are. This can be more likely when dealing with cross-functional change activities, as work standards and reporting can be subtly different.

6 This question may seem obvious; however, is the impact of this change on you clear to those around you? For example, at work your customer service levels could suffer, while outside work your behaviour may change. If your colleagues, clients, loved ones and friends do not know of the new circumstances you are tackling then they may wonder why you are different.

7 An important question which, if you don't address it, could leave you frustrated, or worse, later on. If you think there are alternative ways the change(s) could be handled then offer your suggestions.

8 The earlier you recognize what might challenge you, the better prepared you can be and, more significantly, the greater your chances of making a success of the change.

9 Through the good, difficult and bad times you may go through during change, having a support team or network can be extremely beneficial, as long as you share the ups as well as the downs!

10 A clue is in question 9 but you cannot solely rely on others, so be clear about your performance criteria and don't forget to recognize your achievements and give them the same recognition as you would do for disappointments.

Coping with change will bring with it a kaleidoscope of emotions, challenges and surprises! Therefore to cope with change you may find it helpful to have other things in your life to which you can escape, or rewards that you can enjoy, and so recharge yourself. So no matter if you are tackling a minor or major change do not forget to pause, whether that means for a cup of tea (or coffee) or having a few hours absorbed in something other than the change you have been working on.

Try it now

Sometimes our mind and emotions can benefit from a rest rather than an unproductive slog of trying to solve something, so write yourself a list of simple things you would consider as rewards and brief respites.

Keep the list close to hand and when things are getting tough or you are struggling with a problem then pick something from the list. Beware though that you don't lose your tenacity or disappear and let your team-mates or colleagues down.

Similarly if things have gone really well, don't forget those who helped you and let them know of your success. 'Thank You' can be two of the nicest words that people can hear. This can be particularly beneficial if you are working with people who are new to you and you are looking to build good relations with them.

Finding the balance between being useful and being used can be difficult. Most of us like to help others and in a team environment it is not uncommon to help out our team-mates. The thing not to forget is what your role and responsibilities are.

Case study

Take the case of Paul. Six months into his second job after leaving college the department he was in was transferred to report to a different director. The change brought with it new expectations in performance plus new ways of working. Paul was comfortable with new ways of working as this was more in line with the way he had worked at his previous job. However, he was concerned that he might not be able to reach the performance levels now expected because of the way the people new to him were working.

For example, Brenda and Gary were stalwarts of the company and had grown up with some of the bosses so they acted as if they were immune to change. Paul had developed a reputation for being helpful and as someone who valued delivering his work on time. Recently Helen, his boss, had commented to him about a few minor errors and missing aspects from the Newhaven Project. They were nothing that she was going to take issue with; nonetheless Paul was concerned about the errors as he was hoping to be promoted to team leader in the next four months.

Paul's response to Helen about the minor errors was that he had not quite finished the work because (i) he had to spend more time helping Brenda with a process step she was stuck on and (ii) Gary had said it wasn't necessary to finish some of the statistical work. What Paul did not expect was to hear Helen say that the process change should not have been an issue because Brenda had been trained in the work before it was computerized, and that Gary had opposed the statistical changes!

Paul had been crestfallen and worried about the project for a few days before deciding to meet with Helen. He was working with some experienced individuals who knew how to play the system and had already demonstrated their skills at resisting change. For Helen it was important that Paul stepped up his game, not only because she recognized his talent but she had a personal reason too.

The meeting started well; Paul had clearly come prepared with notes he wanted to go through. However, as Helen began to talk through a number of points, Paul's shoulders rounded and his head began to drop. This disappointed Helen as she was expecting to have an adult 'peer-to-peer' conversation, and she needed him to stay positive. From Paul's perspective he felt like he had when he was speaking with Gary, yet he knew that Helen was an ally so he shouldn't feel threatened. (Case Study continues on next page.)

Remember this

Don't be afraid to seek more than one opinion or to seek advice from those who you report to. Asking for verification or double checking your approach and/or decision is OK as long as you don't do it too often!

Similarly, as well as checking occasionally that what you are doing is OK, make sure that the project (change) is progressing as it should. Also consider letting your boss know that if they need any assistance you're interested in helping. These approaches can really help to develop good relations and prevent unpleasant surprises; just make sure you do not over extend yourself.

Key idea

Managing relationship boundaries is the responsibility of those involved in the relationship. Whilst shyness or inhibitions may restrict your willingness to engage in communications, they should not stop your ability to think and seek support if you have ideas and suggestions for improvements to a situation you are involved in. Equally, if you are of a more aggressive or abrasive disposition, then you have a responsibility not to offend, overpower or intimidate others.

To state this more simply, you should be clear about your relationship boundaries and the connectivity between responsibility and power. This is especially true when entering new relationships or when relationships are becoming uncomfortable.

In 1968 Stephen Karpman wrote an article 'Fairy Tales and Script Drama Analysis', in which he first described the

Karpman Drama Triangle. This model proposes three habitual psychological roles that people often adopt:

▶ The *Victim* is the person who is treated as, or accepts the role of being vulnerable, inadequate or powerless.

▶ The *Persecutor* is the person who pressures, coerces or *persecutes* the victim. Often the persecutor does not appreciate their own power and the negative and/or destructive impact it has.

▶ The *Rescuer* is the person who intervenes, often with the intent to either help the situation or those who are vulnerable, and invariably ends up becoming too involved to the extent of doing a lot of the work so ending up feeling 'hard done by'.

Remember this

Karpman Drama Triangle

The *Victim* should own their vulnerability, take responsibility for themselves and commit to use their power more.

The *Persecutor* should own their power, use it carefully, and not be afraid of it or use it inappropriately.

The *Rescuer* should take responsibility for their power and acknowledge their vulnerabilities.

In the case of Paul, he appeared to move through denial quite early on but then 'rolled around' in the trough of resistance and acceptance. While he believed in himself he was increasingly being influenced by self–doubt, because the people who were new to him were not operating in a way he was familiar (and comfortable) with, and he had not managed to adapt his style to bring the best out of the new situations he was facing. The net result was that he needed external support from Helen.

It is interesting to note that rather than being specific with information on how Paul could deal with his challenge, Helen chose to demonstrate her belief in him by encouraging him to be more curious and challenging. Also she left him free to choose the style and occasions when he practised these changes to his behaviour. The follow up meeting will show Helen the wisdom (or not) of the trust and belief she invested in Paul.

RESISTANCE OR ACCEPTANCE

If you find yourself oscillating between moods or outlooks consider what, if any, resistances you may be experiencing or things you are trying to accept. The change curve is a useful framework within which to explore what can happen as time goes on in the new job.

Moving from the denial through to the acceptance phase is usually indicative of trying to move from the past to the present: the change is happening so embrace it and do not look back; try to stay focused on acceptance and the way forward.

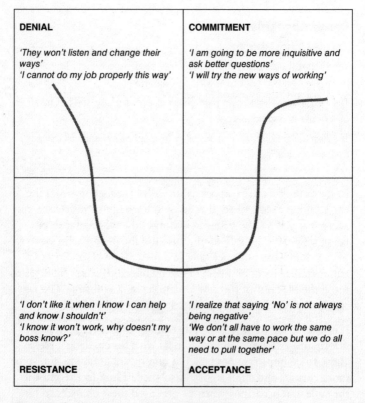

DENIAL

'They won't listen and change their ways'
'I cannot do my job properly this way'

COMMITMENT

'I am going to be more inquisitive and ask better questions'
'I will try the new ways of working'

'I don't like it when I know I can help and know I shouldn't'
'I know it won't work, why doesn't my boss know?'

RESISTANCE

'I realize that saying 'No' is not always being negative'
'We don't all have to work the same way or at the same pace but we do all need to pull together'

ACCEPTANCE

Figure 4.1 The change curve – change caused by others

The case study is a useful example of how changes beyond our control can be multi-faceted and of how you need to manage your moods so that they do not unduly influence other situations detrimentally. Similarly you should gauge the mood of others and how you approach them, especially if you want them to change or agree to things you are going to propose!

CONCLUSION

Below is a short extract of the subsequent conversation between Helen and Paul:

'Out of interest, Paul, since our brief chat have you identified anything that you want help with?'

'Yes,' said Paul, 'Since we've combined with the other function, which Arthur is running, I sometimes feel, sort of, inadequate.'

'Why do you think that is?' asked Helen.

'I'm not sure' replied Paul.

'What differences have you noticed since the change?'

'Hmm. Two come to mind. Most noticeable is there is less energy and optimism from many of Arthur's team; we always had a good 'can do' approach and supported each other. The second thing is that I've become a bit uncertain. The work with Brenda and Gary is an example.'

'Thank you for telling me that, Paul. That was my sense but I wasn't sure quite why. What is important now is that you do not allow your confidence (as a young manager) to slip. Arthur and I see you as a talent for the future. Therefore what I encourage you to do is channel the uncertainty you have into curiosity and be braver in challenging people so that you and they have agreement and clarity over what has to be done. Also I'd like you to keep a simple log of situations where you sense there may be conflict, or potential conflict. In particular pay attention to what you saw, heard and felt. In a month I'd then like to go through your log and I'll send you a meeting invite. In the meantime if you do have a situation you want to discuss then come and see me.'

Paul thanked Helen and left the meeting feeling relieved and invigorated. Helen sat there after the meeting and reflected on it, made a few notes about it and was more optimistic that Paul would be her choice for deputizing for her when she went off on maternity leave. Helen had used the Transition Curve and Model for Moods (below) to prepare for the meeting with Paul.

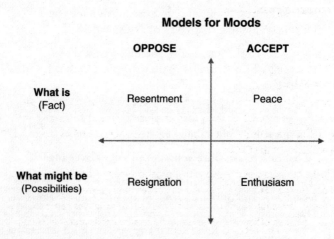

Models for Moods

Figure 4.2 The model for moods

The 'model for moods' in Figure 4.2, adapted from the original devised by Rafael Echeverría in his 1990 book, *On Moods and Emotions*, helps you to recognize if you are in resistance or acceptance. Working through a situation will help you to identify what is **fact** and what are real **possibilities**. It will also help encourage a sense of positivity, enthusiasm and belief because the space you choose to be in is one that is based on facts and possibilities, rather than being focused on resistance.

Try it now

Monitor your moods, both when things are really working and when they're going wrong, and ask yourself:

▶ Is it your heart (emotion) or your head (logic) that is the more dominant?

▶ Do your heart and head need to be more in balance?

▶ Are you feeling sceptical and listless? If so, then ask yourself (i) what you can control that will convince you things will get better and (ii) who you can connect to for support and encouragement.

Case study

Fiona was a highly experienced and competent PA for the CEO of a major advertising company. Fiona was used to a high degree of autonomy and responsibility and dealt with sensitive business issues. At times she carried the authority of the CEO.

After the business was merged with a sister company Fiona had to arrange for the CEO and the Directors' offices to be moved into the sister company's building. Fiona was very concerned that she was going to now work in an open office where others could hear her calls and she would have to share a printer.

Initially she was confident that her boss would see sense and organize for her to have an office or at least her own cubicle. Despite numerous conversations between Fiona and her boss nothing changed until her boss shocked her by announcing that she was leaving and the 'top man' from a major competitor was taking over.

Fiona now faced working for a new boss with their own expectations and ways of working, plus she had to contend with working in an open office within a sister company whose service levels were not at the high level of the old advertising company.

Despite various private chats that Fiona had had with a couple of the Directors she remained convinced her ability to offer the same level of discretion and service to the new CEO was going to be compromised by her working in an open office and sharing equipment, such as the printer.

When the new CEO first met with Fiona she took the opportunity to outline her concerns and how she was used to working. The CEO listened and then made it clear he believed in an open office policy and using shared resources, so counselled her to be more adaptable, understand the bigger picture and, as a member of the senior team, be a good role model.

Key idea

People often shy away from situations where they perceive there could be a difference of view, potential conflict or significant change for them. Having a different point of view is not negative and can create a very positive diverse culture. The key at times in these situations can be our ability to cope with being uncomfortable during change. Managing our preferences and being willing to try something new can lead to new and wonderful experiences that can strengthen our skills and competencies. So if you are in resistance consider your tolerance, accommodation and adaptability to the change and ask yourself what it would take for you to reach a compromise and move into acceptance on the transition curve, then quickly through to commitment.

Try it now

When you are concerned you may be entering into a conflict situation try to adopt the following:

▶ Think about your mood and mindset – be approachable, able and willing to communicate.

▶ Remain calm and LISTEN at all times.

▶ In your communications, be positive, clear and specific.

▶ Encourage the other people involved to be as open and honest as they possibly can, and help them to reflect on what has been the issue.

- Be co-operative but don't be afraid to be challenging as long as it is done in a harmonious style.

- Always finish a discussion with agreement to a way forward – compromise and, hopefully, a solution!

Reflection can be difficult, so consider who you could trust to listen to you talk the situation through. Preferably the trusted person should not only be a good listener but also be able to ask you good questions that will challenge your thinking, so that your direction becomes clearer and more meaningful to you.

Focus points

First impressions – they may not be indelible yet they can certainly affect your decisions, both from the perspective of what you see when an external change affects you and how you are seen to react when someone makes a request of you.

Consider things from the outside in – everyone makes assumptions. Remember it isn't always obvious why something happens. Be aware of people's sensitivities, gain their trust and more may be revealed.

Vitamin C – it's healthy to be Curious, Co-operative, Clear and able to Compromise.

Mindset management – manage your moods and don't let your moods manage you!

Next steps

Over the next few chapters you will learn how to deal with some typical change scenarios, including external changes to a business and management-imposed changes, and we will delve further into how to cope when teams are merged. The perspectives offered in the following chapters can help you to anticipate, prepare for and deal with any changes you may be facing.

5

External changes on organization

In this chapter you will learn:

- ▶ *About external changes*
- ▶ *The importance of effective communication*
- ▶ *How to think ahead*

Self-assessment

Think of your current situation and answer the following questions:

1 Is this a well-planned external change that has been known about for a while or a crisis that has just occurred?

2 Did the organization expect this change?

3 What are the likely implications of this change on the organization?

4 Is this a change for the overall organization or just your department?

5 How effectively is the planned change being executed at present?

6 How objectively are you looking at this external change?

7 What are the implications on you personally?

8 How do you tend to react in a crisis?

9 What makes something a crisis for you?

10 How do you manage stress?

Answers

1 Depending on how and when a change occurs can make a difference to how you react. If the situation is something that is planned and known about, e.g. a change in government legislation which has an impact on your organization, it is likely that there will be internal plans in place as to how it is managed. However, if the change is an external crisis that no one could have foreseen, e.g. a flood or a fire, then it is less likely that people are prepared for it.

2 People in an organization should be more likely to be able to manage change effectively if it's something that is expected. For example, in an economic downturn where the organization has to undertake drastic cost cutting, then it is likely that there may be redundancies. That does not mean employees will agree with this, but they can at least be mentally prepared for the situation.

3 The implications of an external change imposed on an organization can be massive both in terms of time and cost. For example, in 2011 the Treasury decided to change the composition of 5p and 10p coins, from cupro-nickel alloy to nickel-plated steel, resulting in an increase in their thickness from 1.7 mm to 1.9 mm. This small change seems likely to cost the vending machine industry over £40 million to adapt all their vending machines.

4 Understanding who is affected by the external change will help you put it into context and recognize why others may not be bothered or as concerned as you may be. For example, when a legal change was implemented that related to the selling of financial services, it meant that all customer enquiry staff who handled applications for loans or credit cards in a bank, had to read out a standard statement to customers regarding their rights. Those who worked in other back office functions probably had not been affected at all by this change and therefore didn't have empathy.

5 Many large organizations undergoing a series of externally forced changes put in place a detailed change management programme, designed to enable a smooth implementation. Yet in reality, problems may still occur, often because the planners have looked at all the structural changes in the business, but not considered that the managers implementing the changes may not be on board with the process or might require training to deliver the message effectively.

6 Think about the frame of mind that you are in when you hear about a change. Sometimes if you are stressed already, then you are not in a position to think objectively about the change or to ask questions to get the right sense of perspective.

7 The first question that most people will ask upon hearing about a change is 'how does it affect me?' Recognize that the answer to this question may not be known especially if it's a crisis. If the office has burned down, or a situation like 9/11 with worldwide implications has occurred, it's likely that your manager has not yet looked at the impact on everyone, and may be feeling quite helpless.

8 Consider your natural behaviour preference in a crisis. As a human being your 'fight or flight' response is likely to kick in initially, as mentioned in Chapter 2, unless you consciously take a moment to stop, breathe and consider your response.

9 A crisis refers not necessarily to a traumatic situation or event, but to a person's reaction to an event. One person might be deeply affected by an event, while another individual suffers little or no ill effects. It is not always possible to predict how you will react to an event until it happens, however, disaster expert Professor Anie Kalayjian says that the ability to live in the moment and react based strictly on what is *present* is among the most important factors in handling a crisis of any type. This stops you from panicking about what could happen, rather than focusing on what is happening.

10 Stress is a factor that will be present in any change situation, particularly if it's an external change outside your control. Stress can be both positive and negative depending on how you manage it, so being able to recognize and manage stress will be useful.

An external change that affects an organization is likely to be either a planned change with a strategy devised in advance which is ready to be implemented, or a crisis that is unforeseen and has to be dealt with at the time. Many organizations have also carried out scenario planning for the unforeseen situation so that they can be more prepared for it should it ever happen.

If you are someone in the organization who is at the 'sharp end' and may have a limited level of influence you might have a feeling of helplessness as decisions are taken which are outside your control, and you have to just accept the change rather than being involved in it.

Remember this

Resistance can simply be a fear of the unknown. Make sure you focus on the present and what is 'current reality' rather than 'possible unknowns'.

Case study

Mary works in a medium-sized business that operates a number of children's daycare centres across the UK. This sector has to abide by regulations put in place by the government. When a series of changes were introduced, including a national curriculum for 0–5 year olds, the daycare provider had to adapt its operations to be in line with new government policy. This meant that Mary was required to have a greater knowledge and understanding of child development and learn new methods of planning and record keeping. An air of trepidation surrounded the changes, especially as some of the more experienced staff felt that this was reinventing the wheel and they were not sure what the benefits would be. In some locations, the nervousness spiralled into a greater sense of fear about the unknown in general, which threatened to impact on staff morale overall.

Eventually, the local authority provided briefings and plenty of information to staff as to both WHAT was changing, but more importantly WHY the policy was changing, and what the benefits would be to both children and the staff. This helped to ensure that Mary understood the reason for the external change and how it would be of benefit to her personally.

Key idea

In a situation where you cannot control many of the variables, it is important to focus on what you can control rather than what you cannot. Often people spend too much time worrying about situations that are not within their control. This serves no useful purpose.

Mary perhaps mistakenly assumed that her manager knew more than she did, yet no two people ever have the same perspective on a situation. By asking questions, you can find out more about *current reality* and also what resources you may or may not have control over.

Rumours can also fan individuals' fears extremely quickly and if managers do not provide sufficient information to either confirm or deny the rumours, they are likely to just get stronger.

Rather than passing rumours on, one positive behaviour is to ask your manager. For example, 'Nobody tells me what's going on here' can be rephrased into 'I'd like to be informed about....' This simple action, if repeated regularly, can help you get the information you need, as well as shift your outlook from negative to positive. It takes the focus away from the 'imagined future' with all the inherent possibilities and fears, to what is actually happening now and how you can deal with it.

In Figure 5.1 you can observe the impact that external changes can have in the context of the change curve.

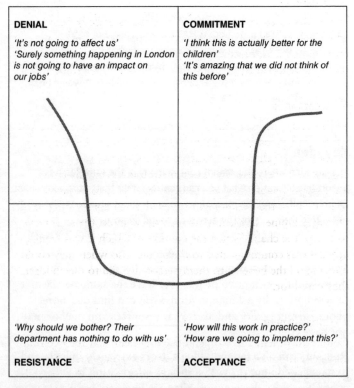

Figure 5.1 The change curve – external changes

▶ Denial

It could be argued that when a major external change hits an organization, either because of legislative changes or an 'act of God', there is very little that could have been done to prevent it happening in the first place. Some organizations operate in a state of denial, with no crisis management plan or scenario planning exercises carried out. This often means that when something threatens the organization from an external source, the effect is noticeable with the organization taking a long time to recover from the situation. In the case study Mary and her colleagues did not seem keen to take any action, until the implication of the government policy changes were outlined to them.

▶ Resistance

There was an element of resistance in the case study example when only the task was explained to staff. If a change is not put into context and, most importantly, the WHY is explained, very often the reaction from any staff will be one of resistance.

▶ Acceptance

At this stage, the new future is communicated to everyone, and whilst employees may not like it, they have a choice. Continue to resist and if there are enough resisters, it may cause the change to be delayed. The example of the vending machine industry highlights this, as operators are likely to be given extra time to adapt their equipment rather than all conforming to the official deadline. In the daycare centre example, the staff began to accept the change when the context in which it was being applied was communicated to them, and also when they could understand the benefits to them personally and to the children they cared for.

▶ Commitment

Commitment tends to happen once it is clear that the external changes cannot be undone, i.e. there is no going back. The government makes the policy change, and therefore it has to be implemented, or the hurricane hits the building and it does not exist anymore, so the new situation becomes the current reality.

As an individual moves through these four stages of change one of the factors that fluctuates is how they view the issue of time. For example, in denial, a person is *in time*, i.e. in the present, and has no desire to look to the future or the past. Then once in resistance, they are observing the past and resisting the future. Once they move to acceptance, they are beginning to consider the future and work out what needs to happen in order to make the changes, and when in the commitment phase, they are often back *in time*.

Key idea

Think about how you view the concept of time in relation to change. Are you present 'in time' or looking 'through time'?

▶ In Time

When someone is *in time*, they are fully engaged in the experience, absorbed even; this is the state to be in to enjoy the moment. They are less likely to be aware of time passing, less likely to plan or stick to a plan and can become sidetracked very easily. (Similar to P preference from MBTI in Chapter 3.) They may have several things on the go at the same time and don't always need completion of one task before starting another. If you think of a person playing a computer game, often they can be unaware of time passing because they are absorbed in the activity.

▶ Through Time

Being *through time* is to be conscious of time passing, to be aware of the interaction of events: time to attend a meeting approaching for instance. It is also to be able to plan, and work to a plan, and to multi-task. If you went to visit a zoo, a through-time approach would be to stand watching the lions in the lion enclosure whilst planning where to go next, this being repeated at the reptile house, aviary, panda enclosure etc. so that by the end of the visit, very little has been experienced in comparison to what's been co-ordinated. Through-time people will like lists, they will always be on time and get angry if others are not, will love to use their organizers and will want to complete things...now! (Similar to J preference from MBTI in Chapter 3.)

Try it now

Think about how you consider time. When you are experiencing a change situation that is external to the organization, how are you relating it to time? Individuals who have the ability to be *in time* and experience reality are generally more able to cope with a crisis situation because they are not worrying about what *could be*.

If you want to not only cope with external changes as they happen, but have a level of awareness of factors that may impact upon your organization, then there are a couple of useful analysis tools that can assist.

The STEEP model helps people think about the broad conditions in which their organization may be operating in the future. It will help to identify significant features and can be used to look at trends that might signify external opportunities or issues for an existing business.

The model will direct you to think about the five broad features of the future environment. First, it directs you to think about the social (S) conditions that will apply; then it prompts you to think about the technological (T); the economic (E); the environmental (E); and, lastly, it will prompt you to think about the likely political conditions (P).

STEEP factor	Major features of the factor	The consequences for the organization
Social		
Consumers' habits and preferences; general and particular attitudes and behaviour.	*Big increase in number of trendy, private flats in central Oxford*	*Style-conscious customers within walking distance so ambience important*
	Young people, single or couples with no children	Customers with high disposable incomes and emphasis on social life
	Increase in binge drinking	Customers may choose to drink, rather than eat out
Technological		
The relevant technology that will be available to customers and to competitors	*Improvements in production and quality of ready-meals*	May provide substitution but does not have same social kudos as eating out
	Technology that links food orders to the kitchen	Can speed up service and ensure consistency
Economic		
The general state of the economy: real wage-rates, disposable income, interest rates, taxation etc	*Oxford economy fairly robust*	Likely to be a stable market of young, free, trendies
	Recession	People eat out occasionally
Environmental		
Latest thinking on environmental matters	*Tighter regulations on waste*	May increase overhead costs for waste disposal
	Food provenance more important to customers	Need to source local ingredients where possible
Political		
The likely political regimes, laws etc.	*Employment law e.g. possible increase in minimum wage and more rights for temporary staff*	May increase staff costs

Example: A restaurant business in Oxford

Remember this

The STEEP model will give you a way of scanning the future in order to consider any external factors that might impact upon the organization and, ultimately, your job.

One situation where planning ahead can be of real benefit to a business is disaster planning. Whilst as a human being, you are often likely to think that disasters will never happen to you, it can make all the difference when a crisis situation arises if you have thought through how the business will maintain continuity of product or service if something disastrous ever happened.

This once-in-a-lifetime situation faced a small business owner, Karen, when riots happened in some parts of London in summer 2011. In the late evening, TV cameras showed a distribution warehouse in north London going up in flames. This warehouse was the compact disc and DVD distribution centre in Enfield and contained stock from many British independent music labels. Karen's company worked with the distribution company and this meant that if they lost most of their stock, it could mean that their clients could potentially go out of business if they had nothing to sell.

She immediately set to work considering contingency plans that related to securing alternative supply, contacting the insurance company, and ensuring her staff kept the customers informed. Luckily, the distribution centre had a detailed disaster recovery plan that they actioned quickly which helped many of the smaller businesses that were affected. As a leader, Karen took on the responsibility to consider the strategic implications, and her employees were kept busy contacting the clients and helping them get as much information as possible. It meant long hours and a high degree of flexibility from everyone to make sure that financial risks were minimized as much as possible. Karen informed her team about the potential implications for the company and everyone trusted that she would find the best way forward, whilst they focused on trying to help recover the situation as quickly as possible. Most of the employees had worked in the company for a long period of time and had a high degree of trust in the management.

Remember this

You have the ability to make a difference, no matter what level you are at in an organization. Make sure you do the job allocated to you, and do it well, and if no one is co-ordinating the situation, you also have the ability to think and take a lead.

In stressful situations like this, some people can step up and become leaders even if that is not their role normally, whilst others crumble and become ineffective, as they get caught up in their emotions. In our busy lives, there are many situations that can cause an unnecessary stress response in our bodies. This may be an adrenaline rush which impacts on our heart, lungs, brain, stomach and muscles. However, the brain cannot distinguish between a real and imagined event and, therefore, sometimes just the anticipation of a stressful situation, or worrying about what might happen in future, can be enough to get the heart racing.

Key idea

According to business psychologist, Sue Firth (Firth, 2009), there are four stress states that you can find yourself in. If they become unhelpful, the solution is to change your physical state, not just your thoughts.

▶ Active: Positive – feel happy, have a buzz, hyper

▶ Active: Unhappy – irritable, grumpy, angry

▶ Relaxed: Positive – happy, relaxed, calm

▶ Relaxed: Unhappy – lethargic, apathetic, depressed

So if you experience symptoms of stress in relation to external events, think about what you might be able to do to adapt to the situation. Some questions to ask yourself are:

1 What can I change about this situation?

2 What is outside my control?

3 What (if any) is my part in creating this situation?

4 How can I view this situation in a different way?

5 What previous experience do I have that would help me deal with this situation?

Once you can find an element of control, it can be an excellent way of reducing the stress. In the example of Karen's business, her employees sought to minimize their personal levels of stress by taking on lots of tasks that gave them a sense of purpose in helping their customers. They trusted that Karen would come up with a plan that would help the company, and their customers, to survive the incident.

Focus points

▶ Consider whether the external change is a planned change or an unplanned one

▶ Lack of information can cause stress so make sure you are as informed as possible about what is going on

▶ Be aware of how you focus on time, in relation to thinking about change

▶ Your boss may not have all the answers so prepare for the future yourself by thinking about wider issues facing your organization

▶ Minimize stress by focusing on what you can control

Next steps

In the next chapter you will learn what to do when your boss imposes changes to your work and how you cope with this situation. It's often hard to manage upwards, so the chapter will provide some useful strategies to help you begin to influence your boss more effectively.

6

Management-imposed change

In this chapter you will learn:

- ▸ *How to manage upwards*
- ▸ *How to build a better rapport with your boss*
- ▸ *How to influence your boss*
- ▸ *How to prioritize your tasks*

Self-assessment

Think of your current work situation and answer the following questions:

1 What is the reason your boss has made the change?

2 How does it impact on you?

3 Did you get sufficient time to implement the change?

4 How did your boss deliver the request?

5 Does your boss understand the implications for you?

6 Who else is affected?

7 Are you being asked to do something that is unreasonable?

8 Is this a change that has been imposed on your boss?

9 If you disagree, is it worth challenging your boss?

10 What could you do to avoid this happening too regularly?

Answers

1 It is important to understand the *why* behind any action that you are given by your boss, because without it, you are likely to be less enthusiastic to take action. As directly asking 'why has this been changed?' might appear confrontational, try asking *what is the reason that this has to be changed?*, which softens the question.

2 When you are given a change to implement, take a moment to think through the impact on you and your other priorities. It's easy to just say yes, and then panic about how you might achieve it, and rather harder to ask a question back to your boss, e.g. 'I am happy to do this for you, and you have also given me quite a few other things to do with similar deadlines. Can you clarify which are most important?'

3 When you are in a position of having no one else to delegate to, it can sometimes feel that you are like the tail of the dog, and are given projects to do with impossible timescales that others earlier on in the process had plenty of time to achieve.

Use the strategy in question 2 to clarify the priorities and also be proactive with others involved in projects to make sure you let them know your expectations of how long a particular task may take. For example, 'if you give me the report for printing by 3pm at the latest, I can make sure it's completed and on your desk first thing tomorrow.'

4 Pay attention to how your boss communicates with you. Some people like explaining the big picture and others prefer the detail and being specific. If your boss is a big picture communicator, it will be worthwhile perhaps clarifying the detail with them before you start out on the task, so that you deliver what they expect.

5 Being able to step into another person's shoes and look at a situation from their perspective is a great skill to master. If you work in a matrix style management structure, sometimes your boss may not be aware of all the tasks you have to accomplish. It's your responsibility to help them become aware of what you have to achieve, and therefore what may not get completed if you have to focus on this change task. So encourage your boss to appreciate your perspective too.

6 When your boss asks you to change something, it is likely that others may be involved too. So make sure you know who else is involved, because if they have actions to take before you complete the final tasks, e.g. they have to change parts of a report before the final version is printed, this will have an impact on you.

7 If your boss asks you to do something that you think is unethical or illegal, there is no requirement to say yes. Think carefully about your own values and morals, and if you feel uncomfortable, one way to address it is to double check what your boss wants you to do, then write it down in a document and ask them to sign it to confirm the request. If they know it's dishonest, they are likely to back down, as you will have evidence that someone higher up the chain than you made the request.

8 Sometimes your boss will also experience this situation, where their boss has imposed a change on them that they cannot refuse to carry out. Knowing this can help make you feel a little

better because you can see that they have been affected by it too.

9 If you disagree with the request – take a moment to evaluate if it's worth challenging your boss. It can be a risky action, but sometimes it will pay off. Consider how you will communicate your points. You could use the EEC model: Experience (this is what I have experienced), Effect (this is the effect and why it does not work) and Change (what I suggest you do differently is). Also, don't give up too soon, as few people are likely to agree to a change instantly, unless you have a really compelling case.

10 Influencing upwards is the key to avoiding too much management-imposed change. Set your boundaries clearly by explaining what your boss should know in order to get the best from you. For example, it might be helpful to say that you are always in before 8 a.m. and if there is a likelihood of things changing that day, an early warning would be good so that you can plan your day accordingly to accommodate the change.

Your boss has a big advantage if they ask to you to change something – as you report to them it is their assumption that you won't say no. However, whilst that may be the case, you do also have some leeway in learning how to manage upwards, so that whilst you still achieve what they want, they learn to become cognisant of what will make it a win–win situation for both parties.

Remember this

You can manage upwards to make any change into a win–win situation.

Take Georgia as an example. She had been working as a PA in a large organization and supported three managers in a regional office. Each of them liked the idea that Georgia was a resource for their department and did not want to hear about all the other work she had to deliver for the other two managers. Consequently, she was struggling to keep up with the workload.

All too often, she would receive a message at the end of the day, with a *last minute* document change to be completed that afternoon. And if she replied that this was not possible, it made her appear inefficient in their eyes.

Georgia was fed up with this so she decided to arrange a meeting with all three managers together. She told them that she was happy to do their work, but that by supporting three of them, it was often difficult to know what the priority was and she did not want to let anyone down. So she suggested that if they ensured they gave work to her by 2 p.m. that day, it helped her have a better chance of completing it. Anything after that time she would not be able to guarantee that it could be achieved. The managers realized that Georgia was trying to help all of them and therefore decided to work more effectively together to ensure she was not swamped by last minute work.

Remember this

You are the only person that has your perspective on what tasks you need to achieve and therefore it's your responsibility to help manage the expectations of others, i.e. your boss and anyone else whom you do work for.

One way to build better rapport with your boss is to notice the representational systems they use. There are three different systems:

▶ **Visual** – you think in pictures. You represent ideas and memories as mental images.

▶ **Auditory** – you think in sounds. It might be a noise or a voice.

▶ **Kinaesthetic** – you represent thoughts as feelings. That might be taste, touch or smell.

Each person has a built-in preference for one of these patterns. The way to notice someone else's preference is to listen to how they communicate. People with a visual preference are likely to use language such as *'that's clear to me'*, or *'I can see the sense in that*'. Those with an auditory preference use language like '*I can hear what you are saying, that sounds good*', and those with kinaesthetic preference might say '*I get the sense of what you are saying*'.

If you recall a meeting you recently had with your boss, how do you remember it? Is it a mental picture or do you recall the sounds and the conversation? Maybe you experience feelings. Once you are familiar with your preference, it's important to notice if it is similar to or different from your boss's preference in thinking. If it's different, then think about how to adapt to their style in order to build greater rapport with them.

Key idea

In order to build greater rapport with your boss, mirror their style of communication rather than always using your own preference.

Often a change imposed by the boss is driven from higher up the organization and they have to accept some of the frustration too. For example, say you have been preparing all the materials for a conference and printing lots of documents, then at the last minute an additional sponsor comes on board who requires their logo to appear on all the documentation. This change potentially has the greatest impact on you as you are responsible for the documentation and now it is all going to have to be changed to incorporate the new sponsor logo. Often the person at the end of the process only looks at how the change will impact on them having to reprint all the conference materials, and not at the bigger picture to consider the financial benefit to the organization as a whole with additional revenues coming in from another sponsor.

If you look at this example using the change curve, again the first two stages are focused on the past and still holding onto what *was* and not what is likely to happen.

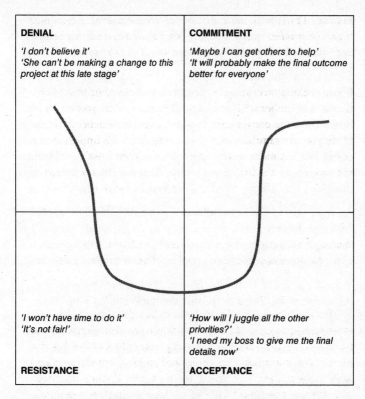

DENIAL	COMMITMENT
'I don't believe it' *'She can't be making a change to this project at this late stage'*	*'Maybe I can get others to help'* *'It will probably make the final outcome better for everyone'*
'I won't have time to do it' *'It's not fair!'* **RESISTANCE**	*'How will I juggle all the other priorities?'* *'I need my boss to give me the final details now'* **ACCEPTANCE**

Figure 6.1 The change curve – management-imposed change

In order to most effectively cope with the impending change, think about what the implications might be for your situation as soon as you get an inkling that the project is likely to change. This means that you can be thinking ahead and considering the specific questions that you may have to ask your boss, or the revised deadlines that you may have to work to if the sponsor comes on board. By doing this advance planning, it means you are likely to appear more in control and organized when your boss asks you to make the changes, rather than getting stressed and panicking because it's all happening at the last minute.

Timing is also a factor to consider. Think about when is the best time to approach your boss with your thoughts or requests if the project is going to change. Notice when and how others speak to them. Is it at the coffee machine, or early in the day or at lunchtime? Sometimes an informal chat at the coffee machine where you offer your suggestions for adapting the programme if the new sponsor comes on board can yield a positive result.

Another effective way to influence upwards is to think about who else influences the boss. They may have friends in other departments whose advice they value, so doing some detective work to observe who these people might be can be beneficial.

Take the story of Caroline. She worked in the training department of a large corporate company, along with her boss, Tom. Generally Tom left her alone to get on with her work arranging venues, and delivering courses and events for staff and managers in the organization. Caroline got good feedback from her course attendees and was highly organized with good attention to detail, so Tom was pleased with her work. Then Caroline heard about a new job that was going to be advertised which appealed to her more than her existing job, so she was keen to apply for it. When she broached the subject with Tom, his initial thoughts were that she was doing such a good job where she was that he would not want to let her go.

So Caroline had to find a way to convince her boss that it would be OK to encourage her to apply. She thought hard about who Tom spoke to, and realized that there was one person he might listen to, whom she knew as well.

There was a group of six people, including Caroline, who regularly went out running at lunchtime and David, the person she thought of, was one of the group. So Caroline made a point of chatting to David on their next run together about this new job she had heard about and how it might be a great opportunity for her. She also dropped into the conversation that she needed Tom's support and was not sure how to get it. David listened and agreed to help. A few days later when Caroline raised the subject again with Tom he seemed to have changed his mind, and said that having thought things through, he would willingly support her application. What Caroline had done was find a way to influence her boss by working out who else could help her.

Remember this

Think about who else influences your boss and if you can enlist their support to help communicate the points that you would like to make.

Try it now

Draw a spider diagram with your boss at the centre and identify the people who influence them. It could be colleagues, friends, suppliers, people in other companies, etc. Then highlight those that you have contact with or know of, so that you can work out what other routes you may have to influence your boss.

Regardless of whether you are successful in influencing your boss over any changes to your work, you are likely to need to prioritize your activities in order to manage your time effectively. One useful tool is to use the 'Urgent vs Important' matrix that was popularized by Dr Stephen Covey (Covey, 2004). There are four quadrants that enable to you categorize your work according to:

1 Urgent and important

2 Important but not urgent

3 Not important but urgent

4 Not important and not urgent

Then using these categories you could ask yourself some questions to help clarify what needs to be focused on, e.g. what are the three most important tasks that only I can do and need to accomplish today? How do these activities add value to the organization? What will give the greatest sense of satisfaction to me if I accomplish them today?

Sometimes there is a temptation to dive straight into dealing with emails (which are often not important and not urgent) but require less thought, and before you know where you are, it's almost lunchtime and the important and urgent tasks are not completed. Then when the middle of the afternoon arrives, and the important tasks are not yet completed, and your boss comes along with a change to a project requiring immediate action, there is no time left to do the important tasks.

If this continues for a few days, stress levels can rise and you are left feeling out of control and with no sense of accomplishment. The temptation is to deal with the immediate, which can ping up in front of us in the form of an email or text message arriving, rather than make the smarter decision to take control of the time yourself. In one organization, an employee was feeling stressed because she had no time to do any quality thinking to address the big projects she had to achieve, as a result of interruptions all day either by emails or people coming to her desk. In the end her boss allowed her to work at home one day per week to get some space and thinking time. However, she still felt that she would be 'on call' for her colleagues because if she did not answer emails immediately they would wonder what she was doing at home. Eventually she realized that if she turned off the audible sound every time an email arrived, she would not be distracted. That one simple action enabled her to work far more effectively both at home and in the office.

Try it now

Take control of your time and prioritize it on a daily basis. Use a tool (Urgent vs Important) to review what needs to be achieved and start with the most important and urgent first. Switch off the email alarm to avoid being distracted.

Changes are unavoidable at work, and if your boss imposes the change it's important to support them in public, even if you personally disagree with the change. You can always have a quiet word with them afterwards to express your views, and make alternative suggestions if that is relevant.

By being organized yourself, thinking ahead to anticipate the implications of change and taking control of your time you can avoid feeling stressed and out of control.

Focus points

Make sure you understand the 'why' behind a change rather than just 'what' you have to do, as it puts the change into context and can reduce anxiety.

Try to think about the bigger picture and how the change impacts on others in the organization not just on you.

Manage upwards to ensure you have a level of influence and don't just feel that you are being dumped on by your boss.

Observe the thinking patterns of others so that greater rapport can be built.

Prioritize your work so that you tackle the important and urgent activities first.

Next steps

In the next chapter, you will learn about teams at work, and the issues that can arise when two teams have to merge. If you are in a team in this situation, you will learn more about how to stake your claim in the new team, by recognizing your strengths, and maximizing your internal PR.

7

Merging teams

In this chapter you will learn:

- ► *About merging teams*
- ► *How to stake your claim in a new team*
- ► *How to recognize your strengths*
- ► *How to maximize your internal PR*

Self-assessment

Think of your current work situation and answer the following questions:

1 Why are the teams being merged?

2 What are the risks to you, of the teams being merged?

3 What are the opportunities for you, of the teams being merged?

4 How well do you know the team that is being merged with your team?

5 What concerns do you have about the merger?

6 How do you want the new team members to perceive you?

7 What aspects of you would you like to change?

8 Who do you need to influence during the merger?

9 What is the ideal role you could play in a team?

10 What support do you think you will need to make the best of the merger for you?

Answers

1 Before forming any strong views on the merger do some due diligence and understand why the merger is taking place, and what it means for the future of the business, the department and you. Clearly colleagues may be negatively affected, which understandably can be upsetting, nonetheless do not allow that emotion to negatively influence your emotional state, judgement or performance. Remember change can create good opportunities, so be alert to these and don't get 'caught out' because you were feeling low and not paying attention.

2 Clearly they can be many or few risks. On learning of the merger and gaining a clear understanding of the reasons for the merger, next do a similar exercise to understand the performance intentions (short and long term goals) for the new team. With that information you can assess the implications for you – base your point of view on facts and not hearsay or the opinions of others,

especially those who are not in an influential, senior position. Now you can form a balanced risk assessment and decide how you can limit the risks on you and how you can perform to the best of your ability.

3 Until you have gone through the exercises in the two answers above you may find it difficult to answer this question with great confidence. Certainly, if you are not co-operative, adaptable, proactive and resilient then the opportunities are most likely going to be few and the first impressions new people may have of you will not be as good as you might like.

4 Using a lesson learned from sport (and warfare) it is best to know your competition so you can better anticipate what they may do and when. In the case of teams being merged it is a good idea to get to know the individuals in the team and, where possible, find out what the team is and is not capable of. Any gaps in ability may create an opportunity for you and you can then volunteer yourself early, so showing yourself to be accepting of the merger and committed to helping it succeed. Anticipate that there may be some resistance from others. Teams under threat, or who have a naturally strong survival instinct, tend to operate more as a tribe than a team, so can be quite harsh.

5 If you have worked your way through the questions so far then hopefully any concerns you have will be well formed. There may also be some which are just based on a feeling you have. It is important that you do not 'bottle up' your concerns and become unduly stressed. Take your concerns to your manager, and make sure to present them in a positive fashion. You'll be able to discuss them and recognize that your manager may not be able to give you the answers because they themselves do not have all the information, so do not judge them too harshly!

6 Many people will simply reply 'as I am'. However, what you might want to consider is what impression you have already created and who in the other team you may be known to. A modern comment is that 'perception is greater than truth', therefore it is worthwhile considering what impressions you create. Decide if there is anything you might need to change

or any action you would like to take to strengthen the 'internal PR' of you around the organization you work in, as well as the external organizations and people you work with.

7   Leading on from the answer to question 6, authenticity is a highly respected value, however, depending on the nature of the merger and how your working life has been in the lead up to it, you may have habits and behaviours which you would like to change. Remember, it is your habits and behaviours, along with your underlying character and moods, that govern the impression you create. Therefore it may be very beneficial to treat the merger as a chance to start afresh and make changes to how you want to be. While first impressions are not indelible they are hard to change and will take extra effort from you to alter.

8   Firstly you need to influence yourself so you are always 'on top of your game'. Those who are making decisions about the merger would be worth influencing positively. How that is achieved will depend largely on the nature and structure of the businesses involved but your line manager and head of function would be two people to have firmly on your side. If they are not then it might be worth considering contingency plans.

There will be another set of people who will be influenced by you and they are your loved ones, family and friends – your support network.

9   At this period of change take the time to think about what ideal role(s) you would like to play in a team and, more specifically, the team you are currently in. Next ask yourself what the decision makers would need to see and know about you for them to consider you for the ideal role or even to create the role. If you do not know the answer(s) then how could you work them out?

Maybe broaden the question to 'Who knows about your aspirations, ambitions and ideal team role?' If your manager and HR team do not know your goal how can they help you to achieve it? In this chapter you will be introduced to team types, which may help you with shaping your ideal role and explaining it.

10 If you are in a proactive mode and have concluded from the above answers that 'Yes, there are things I want and need to do to make the most of this merger for myself' then, as mentioned in previous chapters, do not simply try to do it all on your own. While you are responsible for your own performance consider how your support network and the organization you are in can assist you with knowledge, opportunity and environment in which to exert high performance at this time of transition.

Try it now

Prepare a short verbal personal biography (2–5 minutes long) which you can confidently and enthusiastically give to your new colleagues. The aim of the biography is to:

▶ introduce yourself

▶ highlight your strengths

▶ explain your role and responsibilities

Have some questions ready to ask your new colleagues which will help you to learn more about them. Remember to listen well when they give their answers. Smile, acknowledge what they are saying and be sure to thank them, i.e. create a positive and engaging perception of you.

Set yourself a target to meet, introduce yourself to and find out about all your new colleagues. The quicker you get to know them, the better prepared you can be to perform better.

Remember this

First impressions tend to be long term and can be a lot of work to change. Therefore, invest the time to be well prepared, i.e. clear, engaging and enthusiastic. Practise at home so you are comfortable and authentic with what you are going to say. In the early stages of teams merging there can be opportunities and new ideas formed, which you can take advantage of if you are in the right place at the right time.

Case study

As the sales in a small hi-technology business began to grow, it was decided that one of its sister companies, which was not doing so well, would have the respective sales administration and engineering teams merged.

For the sales administration teams this was fairly straightforward as the small hi-technology business needed more resources and the respective processes were similar. Nonetheless the more enthusiastic sales staff who were willing to learn new process skills found themselves with more responsibility.

In the engineering teams it was more difficult as, although many of the technologies were compatible, the projects were different and well established. The engineering leadership team knew that achieving medium to long term success required them to prevent the two teams from remaining polarized. Therefore the challenge was how to integrate them.

After talking the situation through with the Group HR Director, the engineering team went through a short team building programme which involved a brief psychometric assessment of each individual (including one-to-one feedback), and three half-day workshops. The workshops included learning modules, team building games and breakout sessions to discuss specific work issues.

The result was greater co-operation and, over the ensuing six months, the generation of some new product ideas.

Key idea

There are a number of psychometric assessment tools, and the Belbin team types model is a very popular tool used in team working environments. In the 1970s Dr Meredith Belbin first defined patterns of team role behaviours and over the ensuing ten years developed a simulation for them. A team role is defined by Belbin as '*A tendency to behave, contribute and interrelate with others in a particular way.*' For further information on Belbin team roles, and to undertake an online assessment, visit www.belbin.com.

The 9 Belbin team role types, with a brief description of the typical behaviour of each role, are:

ACTION	SOCIAL	THINKING
Completer Finisher	**Co-ordinator**	**Monitor Evaluator**
often used at the end of a task, to 'polish' and scrutinize the work for errors, subjecting it to the highest standards of quality control	*focus on the team's objectives, draw out team members and delegate work appropriately*	*provide a logical eye, make impartial judgements and weigh up the team's options in a dispassionate way*
Implementer	**Resource Investigator**	**Plant**
plan a practical, workable strategy and carry it out as efficiently as possible	*provide inside knowledge on the opposition and make sure that the team's idea would carry to the world outside the team*	*tend to be highly creative and good at solving problems in unconventional ways*
Shaper	**Teamworker**	**Specialist***
provide the necessary drive to ensure that the team keeps moving and does not lose focus or momentum	*helps the team to gel, using their versatility to identify the work required and complete it on behalf of the team*	*individual with in-depth knowledge of a key area. May have a tendency to focus narrowly on their own subject and prioritize it over the team's progress*

* The role of Specialist was not in the original eight team roles

Dr Meredith Belbin found that the key to teams being successful was having the right balance of team types. So for example, a team with no Plant struggled to come up with the initial spark of an idea with which to push forward. However, once too many Plants were in the team, bad ideas concealed good ones and non-starters were given too much airtime. Similarly, with no Shaper, the team ambled along without drive and direction, missing deadlines. With too many Shapers, in-fighting began and morale was lowered

Figure 7.1 suggests where the team roles may become more valuable during a task or project.

Individuals are likely to have a preference for more than one of the 9 Belbin team roles and there will also be some that they do

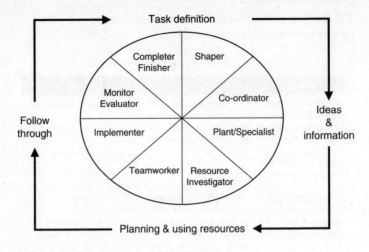

Figure 7.1 Team roles

not have an affinity for. Hence, depending on the situation and your mood, it could be that you will prefer different team roles. By completing a Belbin self-perception inventory you can begin to understand, and therefore anticipate, how you may prefer to behave in different circumstances.

The Belbin self-perception inventory is a questionnaire that takes about 20 minutes to complete. Your scores are interpreted by the Belbin e-interplace programme (developed in 1988 and updated ever since). Your report is then generated, and emailed back to you. Visit www.belbin.com for more information

Remember this

When teams are merging it is a period of change for everyone in the new team and for those responsible for the team, so you are not alone. Try not to be a problem or misfit; seek to be accommodating and adaptable. Show interest and curiosity (see Chapter 6) so you can understand other people and what is going on. If others are struggling and you are seen to be coping and co-operative then you will most likely be remembered favourably, and when good opportunities arise then your name could be considered before others.

Key idea

Building on the Belbin team types and how a task or project might be run, Figure 7.2 shows a Team Impact Wheel, which considers the relation between eight stages of problem solving and the eight original Belbin team types.

Using the Team Impact Wheel (Figure 7.2) against a change process or task/problem you are wanting to solve, you can begin to explore where and when the Belbin team roles could best be deployed and therefore where you may be able to best operate. Also you can anticipate activities you should seek help with or avoid becoming involved in. When working in a team that is being merged try to play to your strengths.

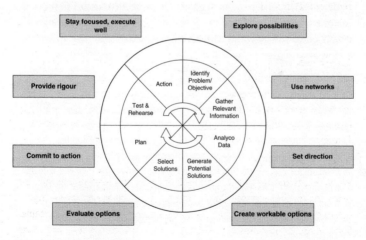

Figure 7.2 Team Impact Wheel

Case study

A new Quality Manager, Eugene, wanted to quickly integrate into both the management team and the business at large. He also wanted his Quality team to integrate with both the engineering and manufacturing teams. Effectively he wanted Quality to merge into the organization so that quality control became a seamless function and was a natural priority for everyone.

He knew this was a big challenge as the business was seeking to achieve ISO9001 and the new range of products being developed would require stringent new internal quality standards.

Eugene's first attempts at integrating Quality met with considerable resistance. However in some areas his efforts met with a degree of success. In pondering why, he realized two things: (i) some people were like-minded and the rapport was strong and (ii) he was able to help others solve some of their problems. He was able to solve problems partly through his knowledge and experience but more likely, he realized, because he was actually doing the work, which was not something he wanted to promote. However, it might be a short term solution to winning more people over.

The more Eugene thought about his analysis the more he realized that both he and his quality team needed to become more useful to the teams rather than appear to be obstacles. This led to Eugene having a couple of off-site meetings with his team to understand their strengths and weaknesses better, as well as to evaluate their ability and appetite to charm people and work more efficiently so they could take on additional challenges.

His solution was to create some learning modules for the Quality staff to learn more about the business. This would mean his team members taking on some work in other areas of the business. Secondly he convinced himself that by taking problems away from departments that were stuck or creating a blockage, he could improve the process, retrain the department then hand the responsibility back. This meant he faced at least 12 months of very hard work but he was confident it could be achieved. Also, it was likely to help his personal goal to become the Quality Director.

Remember this

Merging teams can mean opportunity so try not to dwell on uncertainties and other worries. Show everyone that you are future focused and a team player who wants the team as well as yourself to be a success.

If you have a reputation for helping others while not becoming the victim through overloading yourself (see Chapter 4), then you are likely to be a good team player and possibly a real talent for the future.

While the external perception is that the new merged team is coming together, progress may be slower than expected. The reason for this is invariably that there is a minority (*minority vote* in Figure 7.3) within the team who are still in resistance, and possibly in denial. Often this minority will spend a lot of their thinking time and resources to justify their position. The minority will create doubt, challenge decisions or simply ignore requests, thus creating delay for the majority (*majority vote* in Figure 7.3).

The net affect for the majority is frustration, which in itself will induce negative energy and slow the change momentum further. Therefore, seek to minimize the influence of the minority and try to help them to join the majority as quickly as possible.

Try it now

To try to identify where and when problems may arise in a task or project, and to enable a new team to have a bit of fun, try using the '**Wheel of Curiosity**'.

Using the principles of brainstorming either allocate each team member with one of the seven words listed below or simply keep going around the team allowing each team member to ask one question beginning with one of the seven words listed below.

| WHO | WHAT | WHERE | |
| HOW | WHICH | WHY | WHEN |

The aim of the exercise is to enable people to explore their understanding of the project and think through how the change will occur. It is not intended to be used to be hurtful towards people, so agreeing some guidelines before starting is a good idea.

DENIAL	COMMITMENT
'Why do we need to merge, there is no need?' *'I don't have time to go to the meeting'* *'I need to start looking for a new job'* Awkward (passive or active), either way they won't engage in the change process	*'I'm enjoying being part of this new team'* *'The new team has had some great ideas which we are now working on'* Is working well with new team and learning new things Majority vote
Minority vote	
'Our way is better; why can't they see that?' *'Let me get back to you on that…'* Their resistance can be fed by uncertainty and act as an anchor that slows down progress **RESISTANCE**	*'It's refreshing to share ideas (with new colleagues)'* *'It's worth making the time to get to know everyone (in the new team)'* Embraces being part of a new team and wants to make a positive contribution **ACCEPTANCE**

Figure 7.3 The change curve – merging teams

Focus points

Be prepared – make sure you are organized and don't rely on opinion or ignore things. Make decisions and manage your moods based on facts and balanced thinking so that you know and understand what is going on.

Curiosity and charm – you may also wish to influence what others are thinking which is likely to take skilful curiosity and charm. Watch that you don't overdo it as you may be seen as being a meddler or disruptive.

Know yourself – be realistic and clear about what 'Belbin team type' you prefer and what you would want to be perceived as, whilst also being prepared to be flexible.

Obstacles – often you can see obstacles (yet we rarely consider ourselves to be obstacles!). Merging teams together can be challenging so try to be a resource rather than an obstacle yourself. Help others to get around the problems and you are likely to be seen as helpful.

Communication – during the uncertainty that can surround merging teams, one method of communication that can be particularly effective with your boss is face to face. This helps reinforcement of the underlying messages that you wish to convey, which will also be communicated in body language and tone of voice. Pick an appropriate time and see what happens!

Next steps

The following chapter explores the impact changes to systems and procedures can have on you:

▶ **how you can cope**

▶ **how you can excel**

▶ **what to be aware of**

▶ **and your ability to manage your world in transition and turmoil**

8

New systems and procedures

In this chapter you will learn:

- ▶ *About the impact of new systems and procedures*
- ▶ *How to excel*
- ▶ *What to be aware of*

Self-assessment

Think of your current work situation and answer the following questions:

1 What are the drivers behind the new system or procedure?

2 How is the success of the implementation to be measured?

3 What is likely to change?

4 Who is leading the implementation?

5 Does it impact on you directly or indirectly?

6 What is the timetable for the implementation?

7 How critical is this system or procedure change to your work?

8 What are your current thoughts or feelings about the change?

9 What are the benefits that can be drawn from this change?

10 What will make it successful for you?

Answers

1 Understanding the reason why a new system or procedure is being implemented can put it into a wider context. Sometimes changes are driven by external needs, e.g. legal requirements, which have an impact on all businesses, and at other times they can be driven by a need for improvement internally.

2 There are likely to be strategic measures of success that the organization is aiming to achieve, i.e. cost savings, workforce reduction etc. which will not always be overtly communicated widely. However, regardless of the overall organization's goal, you can always identify some goals that relate to your role in the change. For example, if it's a new procedure for handling invoices, you might start to notice how much quicker it is to process the invoices using the new procedure compared to the old way.

3 Make sure you are clear about what specifically is likely to change. There may be details about a process that you are more familiar with than your boss, so you are in a position to point

out potential benefits or problems to them. Ask questions to establish specifics.

4   Having good leadership whilst a change process is being implemented can make a huge difference. This person should set the direction, keep everyone informed, and be interested in listening and receiving feedback, engaging staff in the change and being seen so that you can speak to them. If it has not been made clear to you who the leader is, ask your manager.

5   Some procedure changes will directly affect your day-to-day job and therefore impact on you greatly. In this situation expect that, during the period of transition, it's likely to take longer to carry out the tasks you do. Sometimes organizations do not allow for this phase and managers get frustrated when a procedure appears to be slower and perhaps some mistakes are made. If this is the case, explain to your manager that this period will not last forever, and you need to be given some leeway in order to adapt to the new way of working. If it's an indirect change, i.e. it's happening to another department whom you liaise with, remember to use the 'stepping into their shoes' exercise described in Chapter 3 so that you can appreciate things from their perspective.

6   Timing is often critical for a system change. It's likely there may be a transition period during which some people are using the new system and the old system concurrently, and then eventually all the data is moved onto the new system. If a timetable has not been communicated to you, then ask the question so that you are aware of what is likely to happen and when the new system will be fully in use.

7   Ask yourself how critical this system or procedure change is to your work. Some questions to consider are: How often do I use this system or procedure – daily, weekly, monthly? What impact does this system have on the achievement of my key performance indicators or goals? If I do not adapt to the change, how will this impact on my job? How important is the successful implementation of this change to my line manager?

8   Knowing yourself and your workplace preferences can help you identify how you are likely to respond to the implementation of a new system or procedure. Assessment tools such as DISC described in this chapter, or the Myers-Briggs Type Indicator® described in Chapter 3, will help you gain insight and understanding as to why some people may find it more stressful than others.

9   It is useful to consider what the benefits are in this type of change situation. Sometimes the overall benefits to the organization will be explained, and ideally your manager should help you to think about what the change will mean in terms of benefits to you personally. Even though some changes appear to have no benefits, it's always a useful exercise to make sure you have an evenly balanced perspective.

10 There can sometimes be some unforeseen successes that come out of a system or procedure implementation. For example, you may end up with a better working relationship with someone than you did before; receive recognition from others more senior in the organization that you did not expect; or the sense of achievement might raise your level of confidence. Sometimes by going through the implementation of a new system and being exposed to new areas of work, you can learn about what you don't like in terms of elements of a job, e.g. sales, or acquire an attention to detail that maybe you did not have before.

Whilst in other chapters you have considered internal changes, this one specifically covers systems and procedures – the results of which often have implications for people in the organization and this is not always considered by those changing the system or procedure.

Case study

Let's look at the experience of Sam who was working in London in a back office admin role for a US based organization. Whilst the operation in the UK was fairly small, the organization operated globally and was going through a period of change with more offices opening in India, China and Australia.

Until that point Sam had had quite a bit of autonomy in his job and focused on supporting the operations in the UK. His line manager spent a lot of time out of the office and was in regular communication with the US headquarters whilst Sam was the one who knew the customers well, ran the customer relationship management system, and carried out the marketing and many other activities.

One day, Sam received an email from the US headquarters informing him that a new marketing strategy was being implemented globally and from now on all his communications had to conform to a particular style. Whilst Sam was happy enough because he liked the new corporate global branding, he was also told that there was a new central customer relationship management database that he would have to use. He was less sure about the benefits that this would bring.

The email stated that all the UK customer information would be copied across to the US database and in future he would have to log on to that system and produce the newsletter and other communications using this new method. Training would be given the following week via an online conference call with all countries to attend.

Sam felt annoyed. He felt that email was not the best way to inform him and now that all communications were to have a global angle rather than a local focus, he thought that his customers might also feel it was a bit impersonal. He rang his manager to find out more.

He was then told that the decision had been taken a couple of weeks ago, and his manager did not foresee a problem – after all, wouldn't it be easier to have consistency across the organization and for everyone to feel part of a global organization. It seemed that Sam was the only one who had thought about what it might be like for their customers to receive communications with a global rather than a local focus.

Try it now

The successful implementation of a new system or procedure should be considered both internally and externally because both are likely to be affected. List in the table on the following page, the impact you think the new system will have on you, your customers, people outside the business and the company as a whole, to give you a wider perspective.

New system or procedure	Impact on me	Impact on customers	Impact on people outside the business	Impact on the company

When new systems are being introduced, everyone who is involved should have the opportunity to input or provide feedback. Whilst you may be unable to change the decision to go ahead with the new system, your experience of using it is of interest to those responsible for the implementation.

Sometimes the smallest change can have a major impact in an organization. For example, in one company undergoing a major culture change, there was a change to the parking procedure. No longer did the company directors get named spaces at the front door of the building. They had to park just like the rest of the employees in any available space in the car park. This small but significant change to the procedures made an instant improvement in morale within the organization.

Try it now

As a user of a system or procedure, you are likely to have a far greater knowledge of how it works that a strategic leader who is tasked to make improvements or cost savings. Never think that the knowledge you have is of no value. Keep a note of ideas that you may have which could improve the process and, if there are opportunities, share them with your line manager or those responsible for making improvements.

According to the United States Environmental Agency, General Electric (GE) applies Lean manufacturing methods in its businesses, which involve a cross-functional team working together using a system called 'Treasure Hunt' to seek cost savings and improvements to processes. A Treasure Hunt lasts three days and allows the staff to view the processes and equipment in an operation. The team includes front line staff, plus representatives from suppliers, government and other stakeholders. In one example, in 2008 a Treasure Hunt was held at Universal Studios in Hollywood (which is part owned by GE). The goals were to:

1 Reduce energy consumption by 20 per cent – $1.4 million.

2 Instil the idea of making energy savings into the culture.

3 Deploy technologies to eliminate waste.

4 Generate a strategic energy plan.

Electricity, water, natural gas, steam, compressed air, waste water and chilled water were considered and although only 12 per cent of the theme park operations were reviewed, the most critical energy and water processes were included, and the teams identified projects which were easily translated to other parts of the operation.

Teams visited sites around the park to assess utility consumption. Some of the areas they looked at were rides like 'Jurassic Park' and 'The Mummy', plus kitchens, office buildings, and attractions such as the 'Terminator' show. Each area had different problems associated with using power. Over the three day period, the cross-functional team identified almost $2 million in potential savings.

Remember this

Most people in an organization only have information about a part of a process or system. By employees working together and sharing information, plus reviewing the process from end to end as in the customers' experience, a business can gain new insight. This requires the participants to be willing to share information, and work together as a team.

In implementing a new system or procedure you are likely to undergo various stages of learning. The 'Learning Stages' model developed by Gordon Training encompasses four stages which have been mapped onto the change curve.

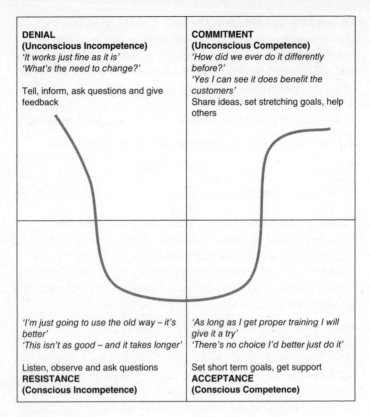

DENIAL **(Unconscious Incompetence)** *'It works just fine as it is'* *'What's the need to change?'* Tell, inform, ask questions and give feedback	**COMMITMENT** **(Unconscious Competence)** *'How did we ever do it differently before?'* *'Yes I can see it does benefit the customers'* Share ideas, set stretching goals, help others
'I'm just going to use the old way – it's better' *'This isn't as good – and it takes longer'* Listen, observe and ask questions **RESISTANCE** **(Conscious Incompetence)**	*'As long as I get proper training I will give it a try'* *'There's no choice I'd better just do it'* Set short term goals, get support **ACCEPTANCE** **(Conscious Competence)**

Figure 8.1 The change curve – using new systems and procedures

▶ Unconscious Incompetence

The individual is not aware of the existence or relevance of the skill area. This is why it links well with the denial phase of the change curve. In our example of a new system being implemented, it is likely that the person has no awareness either of the need for the system to be changed or that they have existing knowledge which could be helpful.

▶ **Conscious incompetence**

In the second stage, the 'what' has been identified (the need to adapt to the new system) and now the individual becomes aware of their deficiency in the skill area and the need to develop competence in it. This is often the trickiest area because it identifies 'weaknesses' which some people tend to avoid focusing on. The resistance element of the change curve fits into this phase well.

▶ **Conscious competence**

At the conscious competence phase, the person needs to learn the 'how' which requires concentration and thinking in order to perform this skill. They have, in effect, accepted that they have to learn the new skill, thus linking in well with the acceptance phase of the change curve. At this stage, repeated practice and support can help the individual to embed the learning. For example, regular use of the new system will result in the skill being developed. What can often happen here is the person rejects the *system* rather than the *learning process* because they don't feel comfortable. They don't believe that repeated practice will take them to the next step of unconscious competence.

▶ **Unconscious competence**

This is when the skill can be easily performed without thinking about it. For example, the system is operated without any conscious thought (second nature) and sometimes can be carried out whilst also doing another task. In this phase the individual can now teach others how to operate the system, although if this instructional phase is delayed over a long period of time, the person can be so used to working on the system unconsciously that they don't find it easy to explain to a colleague how to operate it. Typical comments are 'it just works, and I don't really know how I do it'.

Remember this

When moving from resistance to acceptance in implementing a new system or procedure and it gets tough, perhaps because you recognize your weakness or deficiency, take care to differentiate between the challenge of learning something new, and the system itself. Too often people reject the system, when it's really their own inadequacy that is the issue.

Another element of coping with change in relation to systems implementation is considering how important the change is in relation to your job. Is it a small change that makes minimal impact or the major implementation of a new system that will affect most of your day-to-day work?

Case study

Aziz experienced a major change to his job when the telecoms organization for whom he worked was taken over by a larger player in the market. This was likely to mean changes to the computer system which could greatly impact on his day-to-day customer facing role.

As expected, Aziz found out that his part of the business would have to adopt the system that the other company had used to date, which would mean some major changes and possibly improvements. However, as Aziz relied on the existing system in order to deliver great customer service, he was worried that the change might have a negative impact on this.

The company made an effort to inform everyone about the impending system changes and why they were required, as well as providing in-depth training using various different methods of workbooks, training courses and online simulations. Aziz was even able to study the workbook at home, and was paid overtime for this, as there was no time during his normally hectic day to participate in the training course.

When the switchover day arrived, members of staff from the merged business were on hand to help Aziz and his colleagues to cope with the new system. He felt exhausted by the end of the first week of implementation as there was just so much to think about. They had also discovered a lot of problems with the new system, which was not really compatible with the other programs that his part of the business had been using. So much so that customers began to complain about the longer time taken to process enquiries, which left Aziz feeling dissatisfied, as he always liked to do his best to deliver great service.

Whilst the original intention had been to create a 'one company' ethos to improve operations, Aziz and his colleagues felt that their part of the business had lost out, and certainly Aziz thought he was performing worse than before. It was going to be hard to get used to this new way of working.

Remember this

If there's likely to be a stressful situation at work then make sure you have got some activities outside work that give you a chance to relax and have a change of focus. Often change is about a lack of control, so having a hobby or interest in your spare time, that you are in control of, can bring a greater sense of balance.

Key idea

Knowing yourself and your personality preferences can help you manage change more effectively. For example, the DISC assessment is a tool that helps a person assess which behaviour styles suit them most accurately. The DISC assessment was based on research by Dr William Moulton Marston, who suggested that people express their emotions through four different responses. The four DISC styles stand for Dominance, Influence, Steadiness and Conscientiousness. You can carry out an assessment online to recognize your preference.

DISC PREFERENCES

Dominant people are motivated by power, authority and success and they enjoy getting immediate results. They like to challenge themselves and those around them, and so are likely to drive a system change through, sometimes without too much thought for others.

Those with a strong **Influence** preference are likely to be motivated by being around others and having relationships. They are likely to spend time getting 'buy in' from others when implementing a change, and making sure that they maintain good relations with others.

Steadiness preference people will be motivated by providing help and support, and getting sincere appreciation for their efforts. However, they do tend to avoid change, and may overly accommodate others' preferences.

Conscientious people like rules and regulations and are precise in the way they work. They like reassurance, being part of a group and the opportunity to perform competently. However, they might frustrate the decision making process during change because they prefer to check all the information, preferring to avoid confrontation or conflict.

Try it now

Undertake your own assessment to work out how you behave and your preferred personal style. Then begin to notice the DISC behaviours in others. For example, if someone exhibits the style of an influencer – they will be persuasive, outgoing and talkative – you can understand how to approach them more effectively by matching their preference.

Finally, always make sure you consider the benefits of a systems implementation as well as the potential downsides. There will always be plenty of rumours in the organization when a major systems change is happening, and it is more likely that the negative messages are spread rather than the positive ones.

Some effective questions that you can ask yourself are:

▶ What are the possible benefits to me personally from this change?

▶ If the external environment continues to change at the same rate as it is currently and you do not update the systems, what might the implications be in the longer term?

▶ What can I learn from the implementation of this system or procedure?

▶ How can I maximize my effectiveness even though there are still lots of problems?

According to Putt's Law, technology is dominated by two types of people: those who understand what they do not manage, and those who manage what they do not understand. Whilst with the former, there may be limited opportunities to influence the implementation of a new technology, the sooner a person can be committed to the new system, even if it's not the most ideal system, the less stressful it is likely to be, and the greater the chance you will have that people will listen to your suggestions for change, rather than communicating from a place of resistance.

Focus points

If you know a new system or procedure is about to be implemented, anticipate what the implications might be for you personally so that you can be better prepared.

Looking at the situation from a wider perspective can bring greater understanding and acceptance.

The four stages of learning is a process that everyone goes through, so think about where you are and what you need to do in order to move forwards.

Know your personality preference so that you can work out ways to communicate more effectively with others who may be involved in the change.

Next steps

In the next chapter you will learn how to manage the process of change when taking up a new job. It will explain how to develop a 30 day, 90 day, and 6 month plan and how to cope with the challenges of working in a new organization.

9

Starting a new job

In this chapter you will learn:

- ▶ *How to deal with change involved with a new job*
- ▶ *How to develop a 30 day, 90 day and 6 month plan*
- ▶ *About mentors and sponsors*

Self-assessment

Think of your current situation and answer the following questions:

1 Are you starting a different job in an organization where you already work?

2 Is the new job in a different organization?

3 What do you hope to achieve in this new job?

4 How do you think your new manager will measure your success?

5 What is different about this job to any that you have had before?

6 How would you describe the culture of the organization?

7 What support do you have from others in taking on this job?

8 What do you need to find out or learn about this organization?

9 What self-improvements do you want to make whilst in this job?

10 What are your top five challenges?

Answers

1 If you are already known to people within the organization, and are familiar with the culture, the level of change that you experience may not be as great as starting in a completely new business. Also it's likely that others will already have an impression about you and so it may be more difficult to make a positive first impression if they already have some level of expectation and judgement.

2 A new job in a new place enables you to start with a clean slate. The level of change is likely to be massive as there will be a steep learning curve to understand how the business operates, what you are expected to achieve, what the culture is like and finding out if you will fit in. However, you have a great opportunity to make a favourable first impression.

3 When starting a new job, it's vital to consider what you want to achieve in the role. Is it a stepping stone in a career path, or

a means of earning cash whilst you focus on something else? Being clear about your personal objective is important especially when you have some bad days, and you question why you are there. You will then be able to remind yourself of the 'why' that can help you manage yourself better.

4 Being able to look at a situation from a different perspective can help you to understand and influence your manager. The best way to find out is to ask them some questions directly, e.g. what are your expectations of me? How will you measure my success? How do you like to work?

5 Think about whether you look for sameness or difference in a job. Some people will evaluate a job on the basis of similarity, i.e. is it the same as I have done before? That can bring a level of comfort and confidence during the first few days. However, it may be helpful to consider what is different and therefore the areas of potential learning and growth in the new job.

6 If you were to ask an employee, 'how do things get done around here?' the response is likely to reveal the culture, i.e. *the set of shared attitudes, values, goals and practices that characterizes an institution, organization or group*. This is the single most important piece of information that is likely to indicate if you will enjoy working with the organization. If your values are not shared by the organization, e.g. a vegetarian working in an abattoir, then it is very hard to feel good and fit in over a long period of time.

7 Having support from family and friends can enable you to cope more easily with the changes brought about by a new job. Sometimes a new job can impact on them too, as you may have to work longer hours, or get up earlier to travel further, or be away from home occasionally. The sooner you can help them adjust to your new role, the easier it will be to maintain good relationships.

8 Starting in a new organization is a journey of discovery. There can be so much to learn, from the names of your colleagues to the opportunities for development and the results you are expected to achieve. By giving yourself some focus and a plan,

it will help you not be overwhelmed by all the information and experiences.

9 As you move through your career and life, take each new job as an opportunity to learn and develop. That means having your own agenda and being clear about the areas in which you may wish to develop or gain experience. Can you get an opportunity to work in a new function, e.g. moving into sales, or get support to help you gain a professional qualification? Drive your own personal development plan.

10 A new job is not always going to be a bed of roses though. You may be set challenging targets to achieve, or your boss may be demanding; maybe you have to learn how to operate a new system that seems complicated. At the end of the first week, note down what you think the top five challenges are likely to be, and then keep them in mind when you are getting to know your manager, as they are likely to ask you how they can support you, and you will have an idea of what is going to be important.

Starting a new job is a journey of numbers – 1 day, 30 days, 90 days and 6 months. These are likely to be the critical timescales that will focus your manager's mind on whether you were a good choice of employee. In this chapter, you can take that journey and learn about how to cope with the changes that you are likely to face, be prepared to make a favourable impression and also think about what you want to achieve during that time.

Try it now

Ask for a copy of the employee handbook before you start and make sure you read it! You will learn a lot about the company from that one document.

Case study

Take Gemma as an example. She had just graduated and was offered her first job in a small business providing outsourced marketing services.

Whilst Gemma had studied sports science at university and had an outgoing personality, she was not sure that her future destiny was to be achieved by making telephone calls to potential customers all day long. However, the job paid OK and was located fairly close to home, so Gemma set out to make sure that she would gain some useful experience for her future career even if this job was not to last forever.

On the first day, Gemma dressed smartly and arrived promptly at the office. She also took a notebook to keep a log of any important elements of the job that she might forget! Then she smiled and shook hands firmly with her new line manager who then briefed her on what the role would involve. Gemma made sure she asked what his expectations of her were, and if there was an opportunity for any training or development. He seemed a bit put out at that question because he clearly had not given it any thought, but at least the subject was raised.

Whilst Gemma was not even sure she would last for three months, she privately set herself some goals: to overcome her trepidation about making telephone calls, to develop some new skills, and to ensure that her boss would write her a good reference if she was to leave after three months.

With these in mind, Gemma set to work in the business. Before long, she found that she had a good level of confidence when talking to strangers on the telephone, which also helped her chat to guys when she went out with her friends in the evening. She noticed that her boss was a sports fan as he was always reading the back pages of the newspaper at lunch times, and so she made an effort to keep up to date on sport so that they had something in common to talk about other than work issues. Gemma also realized that she had some acquaintances in sailing from her university days that she could introduce to her boss, who had just bought a yacht and was keen to get into the sailing fraternity. By the time she had been there for three months, Gemma actually looked forward to going to work.

Remember this

Set yourself some personal goals when you start a new job so that you are clear about what YOU want to achieve in the role. Use your observational skills to notice what interests your boss so that you can find areas in common, and ask the question about what their expectations are of you.

In Gemma's case, it seems that she moved through the change curve pretty quickly. She felt a slight resistance to the job as it was not in a role that she was used to doing, but quickly accepted that she could still make a success of it in the short term if she took the initiative and made it work for her personally.

PLANNING YOUR JOURNEY

The importance of having your own plan for the journey is not to be underestimated. The table below shows actions to take at the different stages on the journey:

ACTIVITIES	1 day	30 days	90 days	6 months
Promote yourself	Dress to impress and appear confident	Be willing to take on extra assignments or projects	Make sure you can succinctly describe what you have achieved at your 3-month review meeting	Know your strengths but don't try to overcompensate for your weaknesses
Manage others' expectations	Find out what your line manager expects from you	Seek clarity on who is dependent on your work	Identify the needs of those you have to work with and negotiate if you can't fulfil them	Ask your boss if they have received any comments from other departments about your performance
Accelerate learning	Take a notebook to record key information. Find out if there is an induction course.	Listen and ask questions	Attend networking events	Be flexible and seek projects in other departments
Results focus	Ascertain how your boss will measure your success	Know your limits and make sure you can and DO deliver the results agreed	Focus on your boss's priorities and make sure you deliver	Have an informal chat with your boss about what you are doing well and what you need to improve

(Continued)

ACTIVITIES	1 day	30 days	90 days	6 months
Build rela-tionships	Find something in common with your boss or colleagues to build rapport	Take any opportunities to meet your colleagues socially or have a coffee with them	Make sure you know the key people that you need to know – e.g. secretaries, admin staff	Attend networking events to get to know people from other parts of the organization

The changes that Gemma experienced were around her expectations of what was possible to achieve, in addition to earning money, even in the short term.

Remember this

First impressions are indelible, which makes it vital to present yourself in a positive light from day one. Start with an open mind and positive expectations, and leave any baggage from your previous jobs behind so that you can begin with a clean slate.

The change curve is a useful framework within which to explore what can happen as time goes on in the new job.

Key idea

During the denial and resistance phases, individuals are generally looking into the past, and basing their judgement of the new job on their previous experiences at work. They also tend to bring behaviours from the past into the new role – sometimes as a way to challenge their manager but mostly because they are unaware that the culture and accepted behaviours in the new job are different.

The pivotal point is between resistance and acceptance when the focus changes from the past to the future. Some of the factors that can help to accelerate this change are:

▶ Having an open mind

▶ Treating others who behave differently with respect and curiosity

▶ Observing and asking questions before offering your experience

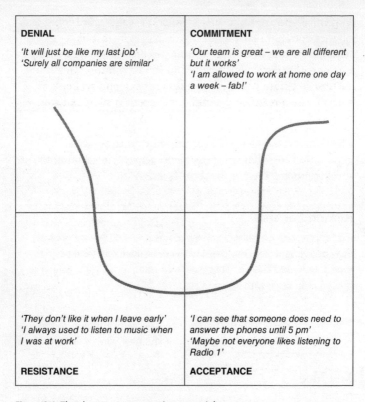

DENIAL	COMMITMENT
'It will just be like my last job' *'Surely all companies are similar'*	*'Our team is great – we are all different but it works'* *'I am allowed to work at home one day a week – fab!'*
'They don't like it when I leave early' *'I always used to listen to music when I was at work'* **RESISTANCE**	*'I can see that someone does need to answer the phones until 5 pm'* *'Maybe not everyone likes listening to Radio 1'* **ACCEPTANCE**

Figure 9.1 The change curve – starting a new job

▶ Trying to quickly understand the culture of the organization

▶ Being prepared to adapt your behaviour

REALITY BITES

Once you have begun to settle into your new job and left behind the past, the reality of how the organization operates will become clear. Sometimes how the job was described in the interview and how it actually shapes up are two different experiences, and it can be disappointing when that happens.

It's likely that after 30 days most people have got a good sense of the new reality. Hopefully the job and the organization are still appealing to you because an eight-hour day can be a real drag when you are somewhere you don't want to be, doing a job that does not really interest you. Not only is it likely to de-motivate you, but those around you probably notice that you are not enthusiastic which will rub off on them too. This is not the time to berate your boss or the company on Facebook as it may cause a reaction you did not expect – a swift exit from your job!

Case study

When George began his new role as an engineer he was excited to make his mark on the organization. Having been told at the interview that this was a forward thinking business with great opportunities for development and international travel, he was keen to expand his horizons. George started along with another new employee and both were briefed by the director on what he expected of them.

Their jobs required them to liaise with several other departments in order to understand the end to end process and how the equipment, which they had to maintain, was used. Whilst George and his fellow engineer, Tony, were enthusiastic and friendly, it quickly became clear that the guys in the technical department had taken an instant dislike to them. Every time they asked for their help, or for some information, they were given the cold shoulder or told that their request may not be fulfilled for a week or so. It seemed that no matter what they did, the technicians did not want to work with them.

George had never experienced this before. He was a likeable character who got on with everyone, and he had never encountered such hostility in any job. Tony and George discussed what they should do, because the reality was that they would not be able to achieve their goals if they did not get co-operation from the technicians.

So they invited the technicians out to the pub for a drink in a bid to build more sociable relations and over a couple of pints, George took his courage in both hands and asked the question. '*Why don't you want to work with us?*' The reply was not what he was expecting at all.

The technicians told them that when the director had advertised the new engineer roles, he had told the technicians that they need not apply as none of them would get the jobs! So the director had unwittingly sabotaged relations even before George and Tony started at the company.

Once this was out in the open, and the technicians realized in the pub that the two engineers were actually decent guys, they changed their behaviour and decided to work with them. And so George learned a difficult lesson *'don't assume that everything is as you think it is'*.

Try it now

Make your own assessment of reality after 30 days. Ask yourself:

▶ What is really going on in this organization?

▶ Does it live up to the marketing hype on the website?

▶ Is this job really going to give me the satisfaction and opportunities I am looking for?

MAKING YOUR MARK

After the first month in a new job if you have an understanding of how the organization operates and you are happy working there, you can begin your longer term strategy to make your mark. The next big milestone that is likely to feature will be 90 days, as often a probationary period will be around three months or longer.

One of the most effective ways to make your mark is to get to know some of the key people. They are often not just the managers or directors, but are more likely to be found in the roles of administration, PA or facilities management, and are likely to work in other departments. In other words, they hold the power to make things happen. If you want to work out who these key people are, then listen, ask questions and observe. Whose name keeps getting mentioned?

Try it now

Set aside half an hour per week to build relationships with key people. Introduce yourself, and find a reason to ask for their help or advice. Generally they like to demonstrate that they have knowledge and power, so stroke their ego. Find out how you can help them.

It's not enough to just get your head down and do a good job and hope that you will be noticed. Learn how to spread the message about what you do, and become known for helping others. By showing that you are willing to take on extra projects or lend a helping hand to someone that is struggling with a deadline, you are demonstrating your capabilities. Of course the danger is that you take on the role of being so helpful that you never get your own results achieved, but you have to watch out for that behaviour and learn to be assertive and say no.

Making your mark can also be achieved in ways that you don't intend. If your manager has set you objectives to achieve, make sure you focus on getting them done. Sometimes new employees are reluctant to ask for help and sit for days struggling to find out the solution to a problem, which they could have solved in a few minutes by just asking for help.

Also, if you make a stupid mistake, own up to it immediately. You can be forgiven if you admit it and the situation can be rectified, but leaving it for someone else to discover is bad news.

In one organization, a new employee had to complete an online form and did not know what to put in one of the boxes, so just left it blank. This caused big problems at the end of the month when it was picked up and meant hours of extra work for a colleague who had to rectify the issue. Don't make your mark by not asking for help!

IMPLEMENTING YOUR PLAN
As you become fully committed to the organization in which you are working, and have sussed out how things work and who the key people are, you can begin to implement your plan to achieve what YOU want. One of the most useful ways to accelerate your career within an organization is to find a mentor or company sponsor to help you. 'Sponsors go beyond giving feedback and advice; they advocate for their mentees and help them gain visibility in the company. They fight to get their protégés to the next level' (Ibarra, Carter and Silva, 2010).

Think about who you admire in the organization – and why? Have they had a fast track trajectory to a senior role and you would like to do that too? Or do they seem to have influence and impact within the organization?

An effective sponsor is going to be proactive and help you gain profile and opportunities, which you may be keen to develop. You may prefer to find a mentor who can guide and support you in your job. Whatever type of person you would like to have on your side, think about what you could offer to them as well as what you want from them.

Remember this

It can be surprising just how willing senior people are to help if you are able to offer them a benefit too. Sometimes in organizations, a mentor can gain a different perspective of the business from their mentee, who may be younger or have fresh thinking to offer. Think about making the relationship a win–win and don't be afraid to ask.

COMMUNICATION IS KEY

As individuals grow in confidence and capability in a new job, having the ability to communicate effectively is paramount to success. This might mean asking tough questions to challenge the line manager, or being able to succinctly present their achievements at the six-month performance review. There can often be an element of self-doubt that creeps in when asking questions in a fairly new role, as people are never sure if they are asking a daft question that they should know the answer to and will be laughed at for not knowing.

A limited level of self-doubt is good. It keeps the brain thinking and reviewing, but too much self-doubt can lead to inaction. It has been known in many businesses that when a new person joins the team and then asks in a meeting what a particular acronym means, most people in the meeting don't know either but have never dared to ask. There can be that internal conflicting conversation – *What if I ask this – will I appear stupid? Maybe, but I don't know what it means. If I ask, will it help others and will I be seen in a helpful manner? Maybe...so what's the worst that can happen...just ask the question then.*

The six-month performance review is an ideal time to practise effective communication skills. It is likely that employees have to review their performance against the objectives they were set when they started at the company. Making sure you have evidence of results is vital, along with any additional actions that were taken, over and above the original goals. Stating the successes in the first person is also important, i.e. I delivered this on time, rather than *we*, so that you can make it clear how you personally contributed to the overall team outputs.

In addition, you are likely to be asked about your development needs or areas where you think you need to improve. Be honest and identify two or three skills that you could learn or behaviours that you could change, and WHY they would help the business as well as you personally.

Key ideas

Useful questions to ask at a six-month performance review include:

1 How have you evaluated my performance?

2 Is there anything I did not achieve that you were expecting from me?

3 Where do you see my career developing in the future?

4 I'd like to find a mentor – can you suggest anyone that you think would be helpful?

Being able to cope with the change into a new job does not need to be difficult if you are clear about what you want to achieve in the job, why you are doing it and being willing to learn and change your own behaviour. It's only through time that you will get a good sense of the culture and decide if the organization fits with your own values and how you work.

Focus points

In a new job, first impressions stick, so make sure that you give the impression you want to.

Have a plan about what you want to achieve in the job, rather than just drifting along.

Be open to developing new working relationships, getting to know people from other departments and finding subjects or areas that you may have in common.

Remember to deliver results. Employees that are all talk and no action will not last long.

A new job is a chance for a new experience. Leave comparisons with previous companies at the door and see how you can fit into the new culture.

Next steps

In the upcoming chapter, you can find out how to cope if you are made redundant in a job, and how to bounce back and search for a new job. If you have been reading this chapter and you are in a new role which is not working out, then the information in the next chapter may also be beneficial to you for future job hunting activities.

10

Redundancy

In this chapter you will learn:

- ▶ *How to deal with redundancy*
- ▶ *How to maintain a positive approach*
- ▶ *About searching for a new job*

Self-assessment

Think of your current work situation and answer the following questions:

1. Why me?

2. How do you feel about it?

3. What are your strengths?

4. What are your constraints and limitations?

5. What did you learn from your last job?

6. What changes would you like to make to your life?

7. How can you use this for personal development?

8. How wide is your network?

9. How are you using social media?

10. What are the key search words that will define you?

Answers

1. It can be very easy to personalize the situation and look inward to you and your performance. Try to focus on the fact that it is your job that has been made redundant, not you.

2. It's natural to feel upset and often it can be hard to make sense of what you're feeling and decide how you want to move forward. It is important not to get too down about yourself – most people face redundancy at some stage. Talk things through with those who are close to you and consider finding out how others have dealt with being made redundant. There are many sources of support, both emotionally and for career transition, so do not panic and make rash decisions. Also do not feel negatively about the company that made you redundant, it will not help. Minimize or, even better, avoid negative feelings as they may show through in your communications.

3. As you begin to start thinking about your next steps be clear about what your strengths are. These can be a great source

of positive energy for you. Although you will want to be busy searching for a new job, which may feel like a job in its own right, you might like to consider doing some voluntary work. Even a few hours a week of volunteering can lead to new contacts, and provide you with social interaction and a sense of usefulness. Also don't forget to include voluntary work on your CV; it will show that you are being proactive and are a positive individual.

4 This is not an opportunity to be negative, rather it is an important reality check. If you are clear about your constraints and limitations then you can better filter the job opportunities you look at. Also you can take a fresh look at them and see if there is something different you can do that will release constraints or improve limitations.

5 During the early stages of redundancy objectivity can be difficult and if negativity about your ex-employer exists, this can stop you recognizing all your achievements and learning in your last job. Recognizing your accomplishments and being able to articulate them positively will help you feel better about yourself and, perhaps just as important, will help you to come over in a far more appealing manner at interview.

6 Redundancy is inevitably a time of change so why not take the opportunity to think outside the box. Before you set your job search strategy and begin your job search campaign allow yourself some time to think about what you would ideally like to do next. Putting in place a clear, appealing and believable strategy is an important first step that will support you through this challenging phase. Regard it as a sales and marketing campaign that promotes you and what you can offer, be that to your new employer or to an investor (if you start your own business).

7 Learning something new is always a good thing to do. Similarly, updating or broadening your skills can be beneficial. In both cases such activities can 'add another string to your bow', show you take your own learning and development very seriously and show you are motivated. This is a chance to take a fresh look at your life and see how this situation can be turned to your

advantage. Maybe you had been thinking about trying a different type of job, re-skilling for a new career or improving your work/ life balance. You now have the opportunity to consider those options and action them.

8 Consider all the people you know, in both work and life, that are part of your network. Think broadly to include parents of your children's friends, acquaintances from the gym or playing sport, or neighbours, etc. Often you will realize that there are many more people who could help you, who you did not initially think of in relation to work.

9 As social networks continue to grow it is vital that you use them to your best advantage. Differentiate your personal and business networks. No matter what social networks you use or whenever you use them, never put anything negative on them. Increasingly recruiters and employers conduct research on candidates which may include looking at social network sources. On a more positive note, consider creating space on the more popular social networks such as LinkedIn, Facebook and Twitter to provide your profile – career history, achievements, education and outline of your career goals.

10 Following on from answers to questions 6–9, as you put information about yourself on the web give careful consideration to what search words you would want to use to help someone find you. Apply this principle the other way too, and conduct searches for the jobs and career opportunities you are interested in and note which words work best; they'll be the ones you might want to have in your profile.

Redundancy can be one of the biggest challenges you face. It can be very tempting to allow negative feelings to dominate your actions and behaviours. While it is understandable to have feelings of loss and being let down, the most significant fact is that from the moment you become aware of being made redundant, you are starting a new chapter in your life.

Therefore the earlier you adopt a positive and opportunistic approach, the better your chances of creating an appealing vision of what you want to do next, which will help you make a great new start.

As this chapter discusses, there will be ups and downs, but what is so important is that you make sure the ups are more frequent than the downs. Another aspect which is often overlooked is that, in this difficult time, how you manage yourself, in terms of how others perceive you, is vital.

How your behaviour can have an effect, for example:

▶ Your current employer can strengthen your reference

▶ Impressing others in your network can lead to new opportunities or meetings or job interviews

▶ Being upbeat can help those close to you to worry less and perhaps be more confident in supporting you.

Try it now

Bring rigour to your job search campaign – whatever you do, be sure to know what your aim is. Work out your strategy, e.g. identify and regularly check recruitment websites, company websites, recruitment agencies, recruitment social networks, personal networks, etc. Set yourself clear and realistic goals and, most importantly, keep your campaign active – **DO IT, don't let time slip by!**

Your actions should include:

▶ phone calls

▶ emails

▶ meetings

▶ networking events

▶ research (companies, markets and recruiters)

▶ writing and sending CVs (with well-targeted covering letters)

▶ time for personal development (to bridge gaps in skills and experience)

- time to relax plus keep fit and healthy
- and finally, some interviews.

Remember this

Your CV is a living document and the covering letter will most likely be the first thing the reader will view. The letter should highlight your relevant experience, be clear and brief. The CV should be 'fine tuned' to each application.

You may find it helpful to keep a list of all the tasks you've done in your jobs, and to list all your achievements. With the major achievements try to quantify the responsibility you had and the outcomes, i.e. relate your achievements to their impact on the business.

As you think of additional information *do not forget to update the lists*.

Case study

Having had three children and been through one divorce Mary was used to dealing with upheavals and change. But the announcement of redundancies at the call centre she worked in was still a blow as Christmas was less than two months away.

Unlike some of her friends she was not interested in discussing the right or wrongs of the decision; it wouldn't make any difference if she was one of the ones selected for redundancy. Given she'd been there less than 12 months she wouldn't be eligible for redundancy payments.

Therefore she started getting the local papers and asked her mum if she could start looking for jobs on the internet for her. Her mother was happy to help as long as she knew what jobs to look for. 'Oh. Search for office admin, receptionist, PA/secretary, maybe project management,' Mary told her.

Mary was frustrated with the position she was in and wanted to talk to someone so arranged to meet her close friend Vicky. As they chatted about Mary's predicament Vicky asked Mary what she would ideally like to do. This led to recounting stories of what they used to get up to at college and reminded Mary of how she used to love making cakes, taking orders for slices of cake and bringing in the orders every day. 'So why not set up a website and advertise locally?' said Vicky, 'We've got so many corporate offices in a five mile radius of us you could work from home.' Mary now has two jobs working from home. One as a virtual PA and the second running an online business delivering homemade cakes and biscuits to local businesses for their coffee/tea breaks.

Key idea

Resilience is the ability to 'bounce back' from a difficult situation. It can be a major differentiator between people with the same business or technical skills and experience. Resilience can be a key factor that helps some people regain emotional balance (or control) quicker than others. This can often best be seen in the top professional sports men and women who can maintain high performance levels in adverse situations through practice and giving great attention to their own wellbeing.

In a change process you invariably move from one way of working – 'the current state' – to a new way of working which is 'the future state'. Redundancy is probably one of the most stressful transitions individuals go through in business – it is disruptive and challenging, especially to our emotions, behaviours and thoughts (beliefs).

Some of the main characteristics of resilient people are:

▶ **Internal locus of control**. Generally, resilient people tend to believe that the action they take will positively affect the outcome of an event and they will be reluctant to place blame (on external causes).

▶ **Optimism**. Life is full of challenges. While you cannot avoid problems, resilient people will remain open, flexible and willing to adapt to the changes problems may bring.

▶ **Support network**. When dealing with a problem, resilient people will have a network of people to support them and whom they can discuss challenges with.

▶ **Problem solving**. They are able to calmly and rationally find a successful solution to problems.

- **Survivor.** Resilient people will avoid thinking like a victim (of circumstance), rather they will be focused on a positive outcome, even when there are unavoidable negative circumstances.

Remember this

Don't dwell on disappointments. It's difficult to walk forward when you are either looking back or down at the ground. Keep looking forward and believe in your job search campaign strategy. Try to ensure that you give more emotional energy to small achievements than you do to small disappointments. Your support network can remind you how good, respected and valued you are so **don't doubt yourself**.

THREE STAGES OF TRANSITION

There are three stages of transition, which are:

- **Letting go** – in order to move forward unencumbered, you need to let go of the past, i.e. old ways, habits, relationships. This may mean celebrating or marking the past in some way so that you are able to start afresh and be adaptable.

- **Re-orientation** – often this phase can be confusing, uncertain and uncomfortable. However, during this time you can discover new purpose, creativity and optimism which, with a good support network, willingness to change our behaviours and having clear goals, can lead to an exciting future!

- **New start** – successful navigation to making a new start requires that:

  ▷ the past has been resolved and there is no residual negativity

  ▷ there is clarity about the outcome you want

  ▷ there is genuine belief it is a step forward

  ▷ the steps are manageable, achievable and none are skipped!

Case study

Pedro had been with the company for eight years and was a reliable manager who joined the company two years after it was founded. He had not made the executive leadership team, nonetheless he was regularly included in major decision making. His technology knowledge and popularity around the business was valued.

It was therefore quite a surprise when Pedro was asked if he was happy with the company, which he was. The new owners of the business decided to select him for redundancy, which was quite a shock. He spent some time in denial and allowed his sense of loyalty to dominate. Pedro worked right up to his last day and did very little job searching or preparation for his new start.

After leaving work and doing all the jobs at home, Pedro realized he needed and wanted a new challenge. He therefore 'polished up' his CV and began to start more purposefully applying for jobs, all of which he found slightly depressing. He therefore focused more on calling his contacts and was very glad that he had kept the business cards of old contacts going back 10 to 15 years, because through LinkedIn he was able to reconnect with the people.

After meeting his old boss, Pedro began to think differently about his goals and started to look at businesses he had worked at before and at some of the suppliers he had developed good relationships with.

It wasn't long before he had a job offer for a 12-month contract. During that time he kept a number of the other contacts who were interested in him 'warm'. Straight after his first contract ended one of those 'warm' contacts offered him a six-month contract which subsequently led to a permanent job.

Remember this

Keep all your business cards and back up your contacts list regularly. Consider how you use social networks such as LinkedIn to maintain contacts.

With social networks be very careful how you use them, especially when it comes to what comments you post. There has been plenty of media coverage about negative comments being read by employers and causing concern and, occasionally, lawsuits.

Try it now

Review your network of contacts and check that you really have included all the clients, suppliers, ex-colleagues and people you have met either socially or through work.

Next consider how they could help you with your campaign. Maybe they have a new contact for you, a company you could check out, or knowledge about a technology, industry or market that you are interested in. Regularly review this list and update it with new people you come into contact with during your campaign.

From the case study above you can see that, while Pedro showed good confidence immediately after hearing the news, once he had left work he felt alone and exposed. He quickly became irritable, which negatively impacted his ability to execute his strategy well. This led to increased anger and confusion within Pedro, which he usually controlled by throwing himself into his work at home. This hidden behaviour was limiting his ability to genuinely look to the future behaviours he needed to adopt.

After wallowing for a while in a pool of anger and confusion, Pedro was helped by an ex-boss to find a way forward that excited him. Also, through joining a darts team, he found a new purpose and so his friends found him more fun again. This led to Pedro's behaviour quickly becoming more naturally appealing, resulting in more second and third interviews which ultimately gave him a choice of job offers!

Focus points

Rigour – it is too easy to be distracted or allow disappointment to negatively affect your campaign. Maintain a positive outlook. Perhaps treat the journey as a marathon, so be strong of mind and body; do not allow the difficult to beat you.

Plan – allow your plan to be flexible. Work out what you want to do. Create a strategy for how you are going to secure a new job and then action it!

Support – try not to operate in a vacuum. After an emotional blow, people can often retreat inside themselves. Open up to friends and family, get opinions on your new job search ideas, speak to career professionals and be open minded.

Resilience – is a skill that can be developed and operates best when you take very good care of your wellbeing.

Network – keep building and nurturing your business and personal network. It is often the best route for finding the right job.

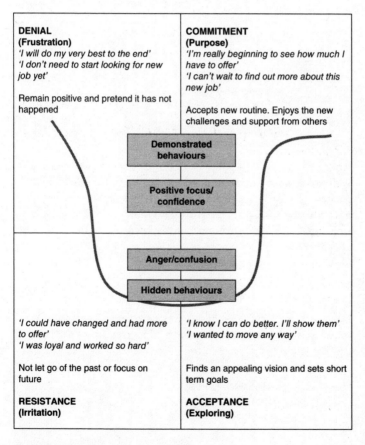

Figure 10.1 The change curve – redundancy

Next steps

In the next chapter you will learn about situations where you may experience major challenges in your job, i.e. you may feel completely overstressed, unable to cope, or it becomes too difficult. The chapter will outline how you can find ways to cope with these job challenges.

11

Job challenges

In this chapter you will learn:

- ► *How to deal with job overload*
- ► *Ways of combating boredom at work*
- ► *How to manage emails efficiently*
- ► *About working for different sizes of organizations*

Self-assessment

Think of your current work situation and answer the following questions:

1 What are the symptoms of your job challenges that others can observe?

2 What would you like to be different about your job?

3 Are you feeling overloaded at work?

4 Are you bored at work and want to do something more challenging?

5 Are you moving from a large organization to a small business or vice versa?

6 Does the amount of email you receive compound this issue?

7 Are you trying to juggle many different priorities?

8 What have you tried so far and what were the results?

9 If you could change just one thing, what would it be?

10 How will you measure progress?

Answers

1 If you are feeling challenged at work, it is likely that others have noticed. Whilst you may think that all 'appears normal', other people can pick up on how you are feeling and behaving. Boredom can manifest itself by silly mistakes being made. Stress often is displayed in health issues, short temper and fatigue. Email overload shows by people getting a delayed response to messages, or a curt response.

2 Having a focus on how you would like the situation to be different will help build energy and commitment for change. For some that energy will come from getting 'away from' the problem or pain, and for others it will come from being focused on going 'towards' a better future.

These 'meta program' preferences are useful as you notice where your energy comes from. These patterns were originally talked about by Neuro-Linguistic Programming (NLP) gurus, Robert Dilts and Judith De Lozier.

No matter your preference, think about what you want to be different; this takes the focus away from the current situation.

3 Overload occurs when job demand exceeds human limits and people have to do too much, in too little time, with too few resources. It is characterized by people experiencing unreasonable workloads, taking fewer days off, a more pressurized workplace, more checking up from the manager, long hours, and unrealistic expectations of what can be achieved with the available time and resource. Sound familiar?

4 Being in a job that provides 'no challenge' can be as challenging as experiencing the overload described in 3. Everyone has seen those who 'coast' at work, and do the minimum required, or are highly capable but in a mundane job because it pays the bills, and would like to find something different, but don't know how to go about it. If you assume that the average person begins their working life at age 21 and retires at 65 it means we might spend over 20 per cent of our lifetime at work. Is that not a good enough reason to make the change? This chapter will explain how to take the appropriate actions to get started.

5 One job challenge that is particularly noticeable is when individuals move from a large organization to a smaller one, or vice versa. Generally there are quite different cultures and ways of operating that require the employee to utilize different skillsets, even though they may be doing nominally the same job. We will explore what these differences are later in this chapter.

6 Email overload must be the number one challenge for many people at work these days. There is the temptation to conform to others' expectations of the promptness of a reply, plus the 'cc.' culture, to cover yourself in case of any comeback, that prevails in many organizations. And then there's the 'always on' behaviour, with employees using smartphones to keep connected even when they are not at work. Some practical strategies to deal with this are in this chapter.

7 The need to juggle a number of varying priorities is something that people working in a portfolio career have to deal with very often. If you work in a large organization, maybe you have to report to several different managers if a matrix structure exists, or are responsible for delivering a variety of projects all with different deadlines. So the ability to keep all the balls in the air, and not drop one, is an important skill these days. Effective time management on a daily basis is a must, plus re-prioritizing to ensure that the activity being worked on is the most important one at that time. The Urgent/Important tool in Chapter 6 can be used for this activity.

8 It's all too easy to get caught up in the detail and busy-ness, without taking a step back to review the situation from a more strategic perspective. Thinking time seems to be a commodity that is in short supply in business these days, and it can be invaluable to help you make better quality decisions, as well as taking an objective look at what you are spending your time on, and evaluating it against both short and long term objectives.

9 There is a feeling of overwhelm that many people experience when the job challenges get too much to handle. It can seem like it's just all too difficult and where would you start to do anything differently. A good question to ask when faced with overwhelm, is 'if I could change just one thing about this situation, right now, what would it be?' Then do that thing, because indecision just adds to the stress and taking action, even if it's not ultimately the most useful action, can help you to regain a feeling of control over the situation.

10 Measuring progress is important to keep you motivated. If you notice that improvements are being made it can bring renewed impetus to maintain the changed behaviour.

This chapter will address a number of areas that can be described as job challenges, i.e. factors that can serve to unsettle you at work. The four areas that this chapter focuses on are:

1 Job overload

2 Boredom at work because it is no longer challenging

3 Email overload

4 Implications of moving to a different size of organization

Firstly if you think about the change curve, it is likely that you are already in stage 2 or 3 (resistance or acceptance) when these issues come to the surface because if you were still in denial you would not notice they were issues!

JOB OVERLOAD

Job overload occurs when you consistently have too much to do in too little time, and limited resources. The experience of James highlights this type of situation. He had been working in a public sector organization for three years in the accounting function. During that time the economic situation had deteriorated, which impacted on the organization and a redundancy programme was announced. In the department where James worked, two of his colleagues, who had been in the organization for a number of years, took advantage of this opportunity and decided to leave. Whilst this suited both of them, it meant that James was left to do the work of three people, as a recruitment freeze was in place.

With finance being critical to the running of the organization, James found himself under increasing pressure. Now everyone was coming to him to chase invoices, check up payment information and ask questions about budgets. He felt under siege. James did generally enjoy his work and therefore had already been putting in a few extra hours every week just to try to stay on top of things. Overtime was not available, and yet he was now expected to do the work of three roles as best he could.

His manager was doing the best he could to keep morale high, and whilst financial rewards were not available, he tried other methods to keep the team focused and motivated. By the end of the week James was so exhausted, he spent most of Saturday morning in bed, and then began to feel tense on Sunday evening about the amount of work that might await him on Monday. His health began to suffer and he was not eating properly. This situation appeared unsustainable, and something was going to give.

Try it now

Job overload can creep up on you, so make sure you keep an eye on this. Try to ask for help in prioritizing if it appears impossible to achieve all the tasks required to be undertaken. Being too ill to work will impact on the organization more in the longer term than making some tough short term decisions to not do some tasks.

These days, in the public sector in particular, there are three factors that together can cause this type of situation – higher expectations of service from customers, greater demands on the organization and limited resources.

And yet whilst the senior leaders know realistically that not everything will be achieved as before, they are sometimes unwilling to take tough decisions to agree what the organization will STOP doing, and so everyone's list of objectives and targets just gets longer. Rebecca Henderson from Harvard Business School has a solution to this situation. She talks about leaders in organizations learning to kill Project 26 – by making tough decisions about what won't get done. Her theory is that most organizations have a list of projects that they would like to achieve, so employees get these projects added to their list of jobs, and the list gets longer (hence at least 26 projects).

Activities just get pushed down the list as new, more critical ones are identified, yet no one ever takes the tough decision to take a project off the list. Everyone knows the project will never happen, but no one is prepared to state it and potentially kill off someone else's idea.

So if you face this situation, try subtly asking your manager to help you prioritize your tasks. Most people go to work to do a good job, and will be prepared to work harder and harder if they can see they are making some sort of progress. Often all that happens is that they feel that they are constantly underachieving which is dissatisfying.

Remember this

Be prepared to make some tough decisions yourself about what tasks do not get completed if you are in an overload situation. But always keep your manager informed so they do not get some nasty surprises in the longer term if they have different expectations.

BOREDOM AT WORK BECAUSE IT'S NO LONGER CHALLENGING

If you were asked **why** you are in your current job, what would the answer be? Are you there just for the money, or is it a stepping stone to your next career move, or maybe there's another reason. Some people are prepared to take on a job that they don't really enjoy because it will give them money to have security and pay rent or a mortgage. Others will stay in a job they don't enjoy because they don't have the motivation to change.

When the economy is in recession, more employees tend to hunker down and stay put, even if they are in a job they don't enjoy, because they perceive that there is too great a risk to move elsewhere or there are fewer suitable jobs on the market.

Your first plan might be to ask for more responsibility in your current job. If you enjoy working in the company and with your colleagues, and you are achieving your objectives, then have an informal conversation with your boss to demonstrate what your strengths are and suggest that you might like additional responsibilities in a particular aspect of your work.

It may be that there is no additional money available to pay you, but by showing your enthusiasm then it may pay off in the long term with other opportunities becoming open to you.

The next option may be to expand your interests outside work to provide some new enjoyment or learning as a compensation for your limited opportunities inside of work. Maybe consider taking up a new hobby or sport to give you additional motivation.

If you do decide to make the move then, whilst there may be risks to moving during a recession, it's also important to have a plan that will enable you to focus on what could be the ideal job for you. List all the factors that are important to you.

Factors to consider	
What do you enjoy?	Do you like solving problems, achieving tasks, providing customer service, managing others, project work etc.?
Location	Where do you want to work? Locally? How far are you prepared to travel? Would you move to another location?
Values	Values are the rules that organizations operate by, e.g. honesty, integrity, excellence, fun, etc, and it's important to find a job that is complementary to your value set
Remuneration	Are you looking for purely financial rewards? Is it a base salary and incentives? Are other factors important – e.g. number of holidays, pension scheme, health cover?
Development opportunities	What are the opportunities to learn new skills, improve your knowledge, or progress your career within the organization?
People	What type of people do you enjoy working for and with? Do you want an inspiring leader? Do you like autonomy or working in a team?

Remember this

You are in control of your destiny so think about what small action you would be prepared to take to go outside your 'comfort zone' and provide a new challenge. Even if it's not at work, it helps you to experience trying new things.

EMAIL OVERLOAD

We will consider this job challenge specifically in relation to the change curve and notice what tends to happen as the individual moves round the curve. Email overload is a curse of the modern day working world and unless you create your own management system and realize that YOU are in control of it, it is likely that the volume of email and expectations of others will leave you stressed, busy and doing nothing much other than responding to emails.

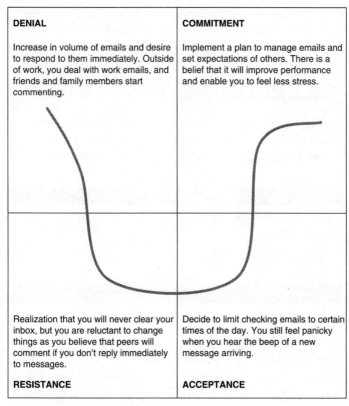

DENIAL	COMMITMENT
Increase in volume of emails and desire to respond to them immediately. Outside of work, you deal with work emails, and friends and family members start commenting.	Implement a plan to manage emails and set expectations of others. There is a belief that it will improve performance and enable you to feel less stress.
Realization that you will never clear your inbox, but you are reluctant to change things as you believe that peers will comment if you don't reply immediately to messages.	Decide to limit checking emails to certain times of the day. You still feel panicky when you hear the beep of a new message arriving.
RESISTANCE	ACCEPTANCE

Figure 11.1 The change curve – email overload

Let's look at the change curve and what may occur.

Here are some practical strategies to tackle the email overload:

1 Switch off the alert that signals the arrival of a message, both on your computer and your smartphone. You do not have to be at the beck and call of others and you won't miss out.

2 Set the expectations of your manager/colleagues/friends and explain that you are implementing a plan to manage your emails and you will only reply to them at certain times of the day.

3 Decide on your priorities for the day, and use those to assess the relative importance of a message when it arrives.

4 Encourage others to speak to you 'face to face' or to call you. You can have a more effective conversation when you are able to glean so much more from their body language or intonation of their voice.

5 When creating an email ensure you make the subject line clear and relevant and state what you want the person to do, e.g. Action required; For information; To be discussed.

Example of vague subject line	Example of clear subject line
SUBJECT: Next week's report	SUBJECT: ACTION REQUIRED – Report for Monday due by 5 p.m. today

If it's to be sent to various people for action:

Vague message:	Clear message:
To: Mary, George, Hugh	To: Mary, George, Hugh
Subject: Completion of marketing report	Subject: Completion of marketing report
Please make sure you all complete your parts of the report which is due by 5 p.m. today	**Mary:** Please confirm graphic on page 1 is OK
	George: Please check numbers in Table 2
	Hugh: FYI – If it requires redesign your project deadline will slip

6 With a forwarded message – be clear about what you want the person to whom you forward the message to do with it. Remove any irrelevant parts of the message. This takes a little of your time, but saves misunderstandings and more time responding to emails later.

7 Respond briefly and suggest – 'please call me if you wish to discuss further'.

MOVING FROM A BIG ORGANIZATION TO A SMALL ONE (OR VICE VERSA)

Another challenge that can manifest itself at work is the change of moving from a large organization to a small one. Often this occurs when a person leaves corporate life and starts up their own small business, or goes to work for someone who is running a small business.

Whilst it may initially seem just the same as before, it is highly likely that fairly soon there are some differences that are highlighted which can make the job challenging.

Situation	Large organization	Small business
Organizational politics	Politics and how to influence is the bedrock of most large organizations. Watch and learn.	Mostly politics has a lesser role compared to large organizations, as there are fewer people and often closer accountability to the business results
Who does what	There are departments to manage IT, HR, Marketing and you have to know who does what in order to get things done.	It's a shock when you have to do it all yourself or almost! No one to fix your PC when it has a problem, so staff quickly learn to be multi-functional, or to have outsourced the functions that they are not skilled in or have no knowledge about.
Culture	Cover your ass…type of culture can prevail where all actions are documented and people copied in, in order to avoid comeback or blame and to defend territories.	Make it happen is the culture in most small businesses, because there is no time for building empires. 'Collaboration' and 'get it done' are generally the watchwords.
Speed of change	Because of the different levels of management, and everyone wanting their say, decision making can be slow, and making changes cumbersome.	Small businesses flourish on their ability to adapt to customer needs, so make sure you are ready for the ride! Procedures are more likely to be in someone's head than written down!
Finances	Large organizations have a budget for everything which will drive focus and behaviour. At the end of the year, there may be a drive to spend any remaining monies so as not to lose them. Therefore a good business case will often get you what you want.	Cash flow is a far more topical issue for a small business, so resources are likely to be limited. If one contract suddenly changes this can have a devastating impact across the entire business.

(Continued)

Situation	Large organization	Small business
Making a difference	Making a difference requires influence so having a good internal network is key. You are unlikely to see the entire process so others involved in the supply chain may impact on your ability to see the overall difference your work makes in the organization.	With a small business, it is likely that you are responsible for an entire process, i.e. you are the marketing department, so you will be directly connected to the customers. It also means there can be nowhere to hide so you have to take responsibility for your actions.

Case study

The case study of Victor highlights some of the differences experienced during a change of jobs to a smaller business. Victor had worked in the headquarters of a multinational corporate for six years. His career had been developing and the next step for him was manager level.

When an appropriate job was advertised with one of their suppliers, a small business building specialist software, he decided to apply for it. It meant less commuting and a chance to manage five staff. One of the hidden benefits was more free time for sport, which he was delighted about because Victor was also a member of the local tennis club and he had missed a lot of training whilst working at the multinational.

The first few weeks were quite a culture shock for Victor. Whilst he did not have to leave home until 8 a.m. – a full hour later than before, which meant he could get to the gym before work – he realized that it was going to be quite different from working in a corporate.

Even after a month no one had given him a formal written contract – it seemed that their part-time HR person had been unavailable when he started and was now caught up in a big unfair dismissal case with another client and had not got round to it. When he started and asked to see the job specifications for his team of programmers, so that he knew what they were expected to do, it seemed that there were no formal job descriptions.

Victor wanted to do a good job and knew that performance appraisals would be an effective way to review work against objectives and then set targets for the future.

Marcus, the owner of the company, told him that he hadn't got round to doing them last year because they had won a big order and it had been all hands to the pump to deliver the software on time. He knew it was something that was important, but maybe not that important at present. So Victor realized he would have to just go with the flow and introduce some of the good HR practices he had experienced, over time.

Remember this

The cultures of large corporates and small businesses are quite different, so be prepared to adapt if you move to a company that is a different size. Watch and ask questions, because often you can add value from bringing a different perspective.

Overall these various job challenges can destabilize you at work, so care should be taken to be aware of the likelihood of any of these situations arising. Thinking ahead and anticipating change, and being clear about what you are in control of, can help you cope. Everyone is willing to step out of their comfort zone if they are likely to get improved performance, greater enjoyment or learning, so think about which one will do it for you.

Focus points

Be prepared for the impact of rising expectations from customers, limited resources and greater demands from employers by making some tough decisions about what work does and does not get done.

Learn to accept a little element of discomfort in your daily work to keep you challenged and able to adapt.

You are in control of your email and when you read and action it. Seize that control and set expectations.

Think about the environment that you are likely to experience if you move from a small to a large organization (or vice versa). Speak to others who have made the transition and learn from their experiences.

Three elements that will help you step out of your comfort zone – performance, enjoyment and learning.

Next steps

In the upcoming chapter, you will learn how to tackle the perfect storm of change – when too many changes hit us all at once. Find out how to cope with this situation and what tools from previous chapters can help you.

12

Too many changes all at once

In this chapter you will learn:

- ▶ *How to manage multiple changes*
- ▶ *About looking after your health and wellbeing*
- ▶ *How to manage priorities*
- ▶ *About the complexity of change*

Self-assessment

Think of your current work situation and answer the following questions:

1 How many changes are happening all at once?

2 How does this experience differ from just dealing with one change at a time?

3 What is the impact on your ability to perform effectively at work?

4 Are there other implications of having to juggle a number of changes at one time?

5 Sometimes this can be stressful for people. How do you deal with stress?

6 What lessons on change that you have learned already, can you apply to this situation?

7 How do you decide which activity to focus on if they are all changing at once?

8 Which elements of each change are within your control?

9 How to you engage others to help or support you at this time?

10 How do you know which issue is the most important?

Answers

1 Think about the number of changes that you are faced with at present. Some of them could be within your department, others may be organization wide, and you may even have some outside work that will impact on you too. By listing them all out, you can get an overview of what you are having to deal with.

2 With only one change at a time, you will be able to assess where on the change curve you are in relation to the issue in hand. It's clearer with only one area of focus. However, when you add in more changes, you may be committed to one, whilst in denial or resistance about another, so it can get very confusing!

3 Think about how these issues affect your day-to-day performance at work. What do others notice about your behaviour? How do you want to be perceived? Make sure you know what the priorities are on a daily basis in order to make sure you remained focused on the right activities for any given moment.

4 If you are juggling, there is a likelihood that a ball may be dropped, and it might be the most important project you are working on. So that is why the answer to question 3 is important. Set your priorities every day, and make sure you only focus on the issues that are within YOUR control.

5 Having some stress management strategies are vital when managing multiple changes. This subject is covered within this chapter and also within Chapter 1.

6 Review the focus points for each previous chapter, and pick out any that you think are particularly relevant to dealing with this issue. Then you will be even better prepared.

7 In this chapter there is an outline of a model of influence and control that can help you identify a way of working out the activities that you are in control of. This stops you worrying about trying to deal with elements of a change that you have no control over or ability to influence.

8 Use the tool explained in this chapter to analyse the tasks that you have an element of control over. Uncertainty will increase stress, and many people worry about what 'might be' rather than 'what is', as explained in Chapter 5. Choose what you are focusing on and what you can achieve.

9 You may feel all alone when faced with multiple change situations, and that you are the only person experiencing them all. Whilst that may be the case, it does not mean that others can't help or support you. Think about who are your trusted friends or colleagues that you could talk to. Sometimes just having someone who will listen can be invaluable.

10 With multiple changes you may feel pulled in all directions and not sure how to prioritize. Use the Urgent/Important tool in Chapter 6 as one method to help decide. Also ask yourself the question, what needs to happen in order for me to become committed to this change? This question will change your focus to the expectation that it is the outcome you want, rather than focusing on the past or resisting.

The threat of change can lead to increased levels of stress, so if you are facing multiple changes it stands to reason that it will be stressful, if not very stressful. Try not to let your work concerns have too great an impact on your personal life. Talk to family and friends about the situation and allow them to help you through it.

It is important to remember that workplace change does not have to create stress and confusion. It can be an opportunity to acquire new skills and, as long as you remain flexible and responsive, you should be able to adapt to the new situation and ensure that you make the most of any new opportunities presented to you.

Try it now

If you are going to stand the best chance of coping effectively, seeing the changes optimistically and being positive about new opportunities, then looking after your health and wellbeing is essential. Exercise is one of the best stress busters so, where possible, try to plan regular sessions at the gym, swimming pool or sports facility of your choice; failing any of those options then taking regular brisk walks can be very beneficial.

Remember this

Don't take things personally. If people criticize you, or unexpected problems arise, this can cause you to feel negative. Acknowledge the stress, keep telling yourself that what you are doing is of value, do some deep breathing and take a short walk; maybe stretch your body too.

Case study

The organization was long established and quite traditional. The business had been bought and sold several times in the previous ten years; therefore coping with change was not unfamiliar to the employees.

Tony was working in the service department and had been seconded from the production support team. His new role involved being the conduit between Sales, Projects, Manufacturing and Service, who conducted the project on-site installations. Tony's role was a pretty invidious one; he was regularly caught in the 'cross-fire' of arguments. Emotions were particularly high when a project was nearing completion because there were invariably delays and people were trying to place the blame elsewhere! Usually Tony could deal well with other people's angst as he recognized the problems as theirs, so did not take such things personally.

Where Tony was finding difficulty was with the increased volume of projects that the business now had to deal with. He prided himself in delivering to schedule, putting in the extra hours if required, monitoring progress and prompting people if things were slipping behind. The latest owners had invested significantly in the business, which was great, but the resulting new product development programme on top of the additional contracts that sales had won meant that Tony's life was now constantly overloaded.

Living on his own and not being interested in alcohol, Tony tended to lead a fairly quiet life outside work, and as he was becoming increasingly exhausted after work, Tony's hobbies of art and triathlons were suffering too. On a trip to a customer project progress meeting Tony's new boss, Gerry, accompanied him. The journey took several hours and before he knew it Tony was opening up to his boss and expressing his frustration at not being able to keep on top of things and now too often unable to anticipate issues.

Gerry listened and offered the occasional comment but said nothing substantial. Tony went into the meeting somewhat frustrated because, having confided in Gerry, he expected some form of support. As they neared the end of the journey home Gerry said, 'I've seen some of your art at the Mill coffee shop – it's very good. Your triathlon times last year were impressive too. Don't let work spoil those talents. Hopefully by rediscovering more of your hobbies you can rekindle your influencing skills. How would you like to develop your thinking about improving the way you work so you are back in better control? I'll leave Friday from 3 p.m. free so let me know tomorrow if you want to come and discuss your ideas further.'

Try it now

Managing your state (emotions) can be a good way to help you change your mood. This is often useful when you are going from one project to another. A simple and easy way to do this is to find yourself a 'sanctuary' where you can take a few minutes on your own, in peace and quiet. Perhaps visit this sanctuary regularly and give yourself a chance to reflect and keep things in a positive perspective.

If you are interested in learning more about state management then there are a number of NLP techniques which you may find helpful for managing and changing your moods.

MANAGING PRIORITIES

When you find yourself having difficulty in breaking down multiple tasks that you have to work on, and everything is high priority or required to be done concurrently, then things can seem impossible. The key is to decide the priorities of all you have to do. Next prepare a list of all the tasks you have to do and try to break them down into the key steps (actions) that need to be taken to complete each task. Make sure you include all the actions which may mean actions done by, or with, other people. This list may be long and the job of preparing it arduous and if that is the case then it confirms the enormity and probably the complexity of the work that faces you, so make sure the list covers everything. You probably won't want to do the list again! Next take a large piece of paper and draw three large circles, one inside the other as shown in Figure 12.1.

Next review each action you have listed and decide which circle to put it in, i.e. decide whether or not you have influence and control of each step (action). Depending on the number of

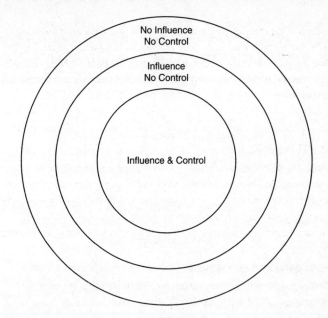

Figure 12.1 Managing priorities

steps you have for each task you may decide that you have to determine your state of influence or control at the task level only.

Once you have allocated the items on the list you can now see where you have influence and control; therefore in the short term you can focus on them.

With the items on the other two circles consider who does have the influence or control and discuss with them how to best take the step or task forward.

Remember this

Change in the workplace is inevitable. So far in this book many different scenarios have been discussed and it has been demonstrated that it is possible for potentially negative change to be handled well and for there to be a positive outcome.

When there are numerous changes taking place the same principles discussed earlier still apply, although the emphasis falls even more keenly on:

► Breaking actions down into short steps rather than long ones where decisions or actions can be paused or stopped.

► Remaining very focused on what has to be changed now and not being distracted by future needs or issues which cannot be resolved now. Obviously if you are dealing with the strategy behind a change then taking a longer term perspective becomes more relevant.

The future is rarely certain and will be influenced by the present so doing things well now will generally have a more positive influence on the future than taking no action!

THE COMPLEXITY OF CHANGE

Having multiple change curves means there are a number of interacting variables to contend with. These variables can be intellectually and emotionally driven.

Imagine that you are involved in more than one change programme. Now you have more change curves to contend with, care needs to be taken so that negatives in one project do not get carried over to another activity. If you in a positive state in one project then trying to carry that over to another is a great thing to do, especially if the second project is struggling!

Remember this

You need to be resilient to move through 'Acceptance' to 'Commitment' and a boost of positive energy gained from regular exercise could be invaluable on those all important steps along the change curves. So, as discussed earlier, try exercising regularly, especially as its significance goes beyond resilience; it also helps to protect your health and wellbeing.

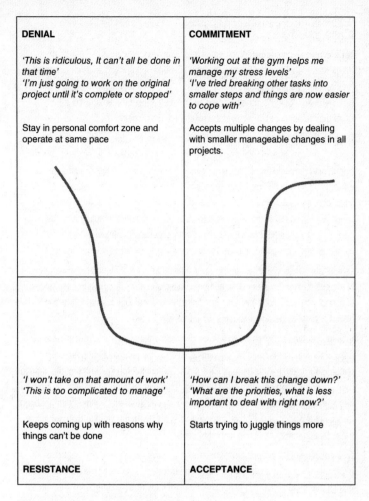

DENIAL	COMMITMENT
'This is ridiculous, It can't all be done in that time' *'I'm just going to work on the original project until it's complete or stopped'*	*'Working out at the gym helps me manage my stress levels'* *'I've tried breaking other tasks into smaller steps and things are now easier to cope with'*
Stay in personal comfort zone and operate at same pace	Accepts multiple changes by dealing with smaller manageable changes in all projects.
'I won't take on that amount of work' *'This is too complicated to manage'*	*'How can I break this change down?'* *'What are the priorities, what is less important to deal with right now?'*
Keeps coming up with reasons why things can't be done	Starts trying to juggle things more
RESISTANCE	**ACCEPTANCE**

Figure 12.2 The change curve – multiple changes

Case study

Take Wendy's experience for example. She was working in corporate hospitality and had to contend with the changing demands of customers and a wide variety of corporate events. She had left school early but studied at night school, then with the Open University, to gain qualifications in catering and business management.

Despite her qualifications Wendy had to start in the corporate hospitality by waiting on tables and working in the kitchens. While Wendy understood the principles of apprenticeships and working her way up, she thought that her experience gained temping at weekends and evenings for a wedding catering business and pub would have counted for more. She very quickly became a team leader so attended the on-site planning meetings. Wendy had natural curiosity which, with her logical mind and previous experience as co-ordinator for a training company, meant she was regularly offering suggestions.

Often her ideas went unrecognized which annoyed her but she refused to let it get to her. She knew that the industry could be quite pressured and she had learned from her mother, who was a county tennis champion, how to stay calm and focused when things 'weren't going your way'.

When she was promoted to event co-ordinator what she found hard to adjust to were the number of changes and the lack of explanation for those changes. It increasingly seemed chaotic which meant people would just do things, often without thinking. This made Wendy reflect on her experience waiting on tables and how her suggestions were often ignored. She talked about it with her mum and with her boss at the pub, who had been head waiter at a top country club.

The conclusion she reached was that she was confident she had the motivation and interpersonal skills to succeed, but that there were three things she had to do for both the business and her to perform better:

▶ create a relationship with her manager and the owner where they were comfortable for her to challenge and seek clarity on changes

▶ introduce a visual planning tool so changes could be easily assessed and discussed

▶ promote a culture shift, so that everyone was more included and encouraged to put forward their ideas and questions.

Wendy enjoyed considerable success and now runs her own successful corporate hospitality business.

Try it now

Drawing on Wendy's case study, what were the essential behaviours?

By coping and demonstrating good 'followership' you can stand out and show that you have the potential to thrive in change. Underlying coping and followership you will need to personally excel at:

▶ *Managing your motivation* – always act optimistically, never publically be negative.

▶ *Demonstrating your abilities* – be proactive and show *all* your abilities and willingness to work outside your comfort zone.

▶ *Regular social interactions* – even when you are busy be willing and able to spend time with others at work. If people like, respect and understand you, there is less likelihood of resistance.

▶ *Being organized and structured* – those who lead and manage change value their team members who are reliable, unflustered, know what they have to do, when and where and are on time.

Work at the four essential behaviours above and note how easier it becomes to influence the thinking and actions of others.

Building on experience of Wendy from the case study above, and the four vital behaviours, let's now look outside the work environment and consider the world of entertainment and one particular entertainer, the juggler!

MULTIPLE CHANGES

Jugglers deal with multiple changes so what lessons can you learn from them?

CONSISTENCY – STABILITY AND PREDICTABILITY

Being consistent gives a juggler the sense of certainty that the next object will be in the right place at the right time. If they don't maintain their posture, breathing and movement to that which they have practised and they know works then it will induce uncertainty. Uncertainty will lead to lowering of confidence, concentration and, ultimately, control.

ACHIEVABLE – REALISTIC SENSE OF PURPOSE

Dropping anything that's being juggled is unacceptable so while there may be danger (juggling knives) or complexity (juggling while moving) a lot of practice will mean that the risk element is minimized to a manageable and acceptable level.

FOCUS – CONTROLLING THE VARIABLES

Practice guides a juggler on what parameters (factors) they have to concentrate on as well as the ones they must master. In business, the chance to practise may not occur and so might be substituted by meetings and discussions. In either situation it is important that you are clear about what the parameters are that influence the changes you are tackling. If you are represented in a meeting or discussion then ensure your representative knows your issues and reports back to you.

CONNECTION – STAYING 'IN TOUCH'

For a juggler this means (i) sensing the feel of the object being juggled – how it feels as it touches their hand and (ii) deciding at what speed to throw it next. The business equivalent is the communications you receive and give.

MEASURABLE – SUCCESS IS SPECIFIC

From childhood onwards, everyone strives for success and to be deprived of it can lead to a downward spiral of confidence. Therefore it should be no surprise that consciously or unconsciously individuals have a deep-seated tendency to gauge their success.

Remember this

Expanding the juggler idea, here are some questions to bear in mind when handling lots of changes.

▶ How can you introduce certainty to the changes you are dealing/coping with?

▶ In the change(s) you are dealing with, how can you minimize the risks so that the tasks can be completed as agreed?

▶ How can you ensure that the variables which affect you remain in focus?

▶ How well do you sense (see, listen and feel) the communications you receive?

> How well do you create and assess the communications you send?

> How do you measure and monitor your changes in terms of success?

Focus points

Health and wellbeing – speak regularly with a confidant about your main pressures at work; do not 'bottle' things up. Keep fit and well nourished. Do not take things personally and manage your stress levels so they are not compromising your performance.

State management – create a 'sanctuary' where you can regularly go to relax, reflect and galvanize yourself. Attend seminars that can help with your personal development, e.g. interpersonal and organizing skills as well as technical skills relevant to your work.

Influence and control – recognize what is within your influence and control and make a conscious effort not to worry about issues that are not within your area of control.

Juggling – change can be difficult; multiple changes are tougher again and often bring greater complexity as well extra challenges. Coping with change takes preparation and discipline. Learning from jugglers; some key aspects to focus on are:

> Consistency – stability and predictability

> Achievable – realistic sense of purpose

> Focus – controlling the variables

> Connection – staying 'in touch'

> Measurable – success is specific

Essential behaviours – If you want to improve your ability to influence then the behaviours you should practise and improve on are:

> Managing your motivation

> Demonstrating your abilities

> Regular social interactions

> Being organized and structured

Next steps

Having considered the various workplace change scenarios in Chapters 4 to 12, you should now be ready to cope better with any change at work that you are likely to face in the future. The change curve model has also given you a framework of understanding about the steps in the change process.

The final two chapters in the book broaden out the issue of coping with change to enable you to be 'change-ready' in future, as well as helping you to think about applying the principles you have learned to any change issues in life outside work.

13

Being ready: anticipating change

In this chapter you will learn:

- ▶ *How to anticipate new changes*
- ▶ *Ways of dealing with intangible changes*

Self-assessment

Think of your current work situation and answer the following questions:

1 What do you currently do in order to anticipate change?

2 How do you deal with a change that may be unlikely to affect you?

3 How do you deal with a change that may impact on what you do?

4 What are the typical signs of impending change?

5 How do you react to a new change?

6 How do you deal with surprises?

7 What can you do to make sure that planned changes do not bring any unexpected surprises?

8 What are the benefits to anticipating change?

9 How can time be found to look ahead and anticipate better?

10 How can you justify a change that you sense the need for, but cannot explain?

Answers

Note: The answers in this chapter are longer than in Chapters 1–12, as links are made to topics discussed previously.

1 In considering what you currently do to anticipate change it is worthwhile noticing whether, overall, you are proactive or reactive. Neither is right or wrong as different situations will require different approaches.

Typically those who are predominantly reactive tend not to be focusing too far ahead and so may often be surprised by change, possibly responding in a negative or neutral manner to it. In trying to notice more of the signs about the future it is helpful to recognize one's preferences for receiving information, i.e. Visual, Auditory or Kinaesthetic (VAK). As we all have a preferred method that we tend to use, the more you work to improve your preparedness to use all three channels, the greater will be your ability to receive information and sense what is going on around you.

Those who are more proactive are likely to have a natural tendency to be regularly scanning the activities that are going on around them, both directly and indirectly, in their own world. Proactivity invariably brings with it a heightened curiosity so proactive people will more naturally be inclined to probe into the future. As discussed earlier, their natural source of awareness will be dominated by their VAK preference.

Useful reading: *Chapter 3 – Past, present and future*
                               Chapter 6 – VAK preferences

2 If you are busy, the temptation will be to do nothing! Your degree of empathy with the change and those in your network who are affected is most likely going to influence your initial reaction. Obviously if you are inclined to help and it is not a change that involves or affects you then ask yourself *'What is the justification for becoming involved?''* Clearly doing something that may detract from the actions and responsibilities you may have, needs careful thought. It is not normally advisable to risk impairing your performance unnecessarily. A possible exception to this might be if, by offering or providing support, you are helping somebody within your team or network. While there is no guarantee, it will hopefully lead to a reciprocal arrangement whereby they may be able to help you in the future.

Consider also that, despite the pressures you may be under, deeper consideration may be very beneficial. Firstly, for example, by making the time to go to your sanctuary and considering who the change will affect and whether there is anything you could do to help them. Your help to them today may be returned at a time when you really need it. Taking time to think through a change that may not directly affect you is a 'safe' opportunity for you to practise using some of the ideas you've gleaned from this book. Practice is what will deliver sustainable improvement.

Useful reading: *Chapter 7 – Team Impact Wheel*
                               Chapter 12 – State Management / Sanctuary

3 Firstly, do not panic or go into denial, rather seek to understand the context and need for the change. Once you understand the change and its ramifications then consider its significance to the other work you have to do, i.e. the relative priority of the new change. Sometimes you may naturally think this through very quickly, however, take the time to ensure it is thought through and not just 'gut reaction'. Often it can be useful to discuss new changes with your boss, especially if you approach the discussion with 'we' in mind and do not convey a sense to your boss of 'I have a problem I want you to help me with'.

Very few people like unpleasant surprises so try to approach your boss with solutions to the situation that you wish to discuss. In this case, it could be that you want to quickly review your workload with your boss in order to ensure that the urgency you are applying to this new change is appropriate for you, as well as for the wider team or function you are operating in.

Useful reading: Chapter 6 – Influence and Control Model
Chapter 12 – State Management/Sanctuary

4 Your acuity will help you to read the signs. Often the signs are the state or mood of those you work with, or possibly of those further afield. Sometimes though, it can be your 'inner voice', i.e. your gut-feeling, that is speaking to you. It is not uncommon with gut-feelings that you find it difficult, sometimes frustratingly so, to explain or justify what you are sensing. When that happens it can be very useful to try to talk through what you are sensing with a trusted colleague or friend. Below are a few examples of where you may be getting clues that are feeding your 'gut-feeling':

▶ people start sending emails rather than speaking with you, suggesting avoidance

▶ people's communications are short and less helpful, suggesting impatience

▶ people's body language is more neutral or sad, suggesting they are under pressure

▶ people's dress is less smart or co-ordinated, suggesting lack of care

In trying to assess what might be happening in a situation you are facing, or that someone else might be facing, consider looking at the circumstances from different perspectives, i.e. perceptual positions. Also if you are trying to look beyond your own immediate surroundings, and identify broader conditions and trends, then perhaps try using the STEEP model.

Useful reading: Chapter 3 – Perceptual Positions
Chapter 5 – STEEP model

5 As mentioned in answer 3 it is so important not to react badly. Where possible, keep a positive mindset – every change brings with it opportunities as well as challenges. Often it is how you deal with the challenges that will have the biggest influence on the opportunities that may come your way.

If the new change does lean you towards a strong emotional state then your ability to think clearly, neutrally and analyse your options may very well be impaired. Being calm and balanced will invariably give you the best chance of a good outcome, so whether it is making time to visit your sanctuary, seeking support from your network or taking a quick walk, it is important to quickly recover a balanced state.

Remember the juggler in Chapter 12: stay focused.

Useful reading: Chapter 1 – Thinking Patterns
Chapter 12 – Juggling

6 The answer to this question may have two parts and be conflicting! How you think you deal with surprises and how others think you deal with them may differ. Therefore, in part, the answer lies in being authentic plus appropriately measured and considered in the reactions and responses you give. Remember, the perceptions others will have of how you deal with surprises is not simply just in what you say. People will form their views of you from the signals you give. For example:

▶ what and how you speak and write

▶ how you look and behave

▶ the timing and energy of your communications

Therefore, when dealing with surprises recognize what the drivers are for any negative senses you may have. If the surprise means dealing with something that is uncomfortable for you, then that in itself is not a reason to be negative. Ask yourself what making the uncomfortable into a comfortable, or at least tolerable, activity would give you. Remember, if the surprise means you are now facing a significant challenge then perhaps consider how your support network can help.

Useful reading: Chapter 4 – Moods
Chapter 5 – Stress states

7 Surprises can be categorized as either expected or unexpected. Expected surprises are ones that, although they may not have been fully anticipated, they had been considered, in some way, as a surprise. The unexpected are surprises for which you have not prepared and usually are the ones that are hardest to initially deal with.

When dealing with planned changes it is likely that our expectations and decisions are based on history and past habits. A consequence of operating from history and habit is that it encourages us to spend too much time in the past. The ability to be adaptable and make improvements is driven from being in the present, regularly evaluating performance and then projecting that forward to assess (i) if it is good enough to achieve the target and (ii) if there are any improvements that can be incorporated.

Therefore one way to help prevent there being surprises with existing changes is to maintain:

▶ healthy stress management levels for you and the change team

▶ an inclusive curiosity which everyone in the team can share

▶ regular performance monitoring of the things that both directly and indirectly affect the work you do

Also remember the attributes of a juggler:

- ▶ consistency – stability and predictability
- ▶ achievable – realistic sense of purpose
- ▶ focus – controlling the variables
- ▶ connection – staying 'in touch'
- ▶ measurable – success is specific

Useful reading: Chapter 1 – Task Performance Curve
Chapter 12 – Juggling

8 A lot of the questions and answers so far have touched in some way on the aspect of surprise in change. Living with surprises, be they expected or unexpected, can become unduly stressful therefore reducing stress by being well prepared and informed about the factors that affect the change will certainly help. Also making time to think forward to try to anticipate where changes, problems or surprises may come from will also help you to remain a calm and balanced state, as well as develop your resilience.

Other benefits of anticipating change are that if you remain approachable, easy to work with, and able to cope with change, then those around you are likely to work better with you, i.e. people are more likely to respect, trust and feel safe with you.

All of which can lead to other people sharing with you their concerns and ideas, which might enable you to be better prepared. Finally anticipating changes will lead you to opportunities for 'win–win' situations rather than 'win–lose/lose–win'. For those who are unprepared they are too often caught off-guard and therefore respond poorly to change; if this results in a 'lose' position then there can be extra work required to re-orientate them back into a positive state.

One useful habit is to practise making regular small changes so that you become familiar with things never being the same. This new habit can lead to a better tolerance when other changes occur.

Useful reading: Chapter 10 – Resilience
Chapter 6 – Win–wins

9 How can time be found to look ahead and anticipate better?

A wise senior manager once said, 'Finding time is difficult, making time is even harder and taking time is easy.' After some reflection his point became clear – being efficient is difficult, creating extra resource is even harder and wasting time is easy!

Therefore the answer to the question of how to improve your ability to look ahead and anticipate (future focus), lies in making future focus part of your routine and priority. When the workload is heavy or the pressure too high then it is not uncommon for there to be a strong tendency in some people to become 'mission orientated' and disregard everything that does not help to produce immediate results. This heightened present focus ultimately can become unhealthy.

When examining a situation you may wish to change, using a combination of the Time Line and Curiosity models can provide a very constructive framework, especially when your mind is full of other issues. The Time Line Model helps you to explore things from the past through to the present and then out into the future. The Curiosity model will help you to create a series of questions to challenge your thinking. Sometimes starting out with a few minutes in your 'sanctuary' mindset to just neutralize thinking can be very helpful in producing a broader, more balanced, outcome.

Useful reading: Chapter 13 – Time Line Model
Chapter 7 – Wheel of Curiosity

10 As mentioned in answer 4 'gut-feelings' can be frustrating to explain, especially when others do not share the same sense. It is at moments like this when others' perception of you can help to transport them towards the belief (gut-feeling) that you have. Given people's perception of you is built around what they think about you – see, hear and feel – and is not totally evidence–based, then how you behave towards them will have a significant impact on their level of respect and trust in you. If their trust and respect is good then they are more likely to (i) be prepared to work with you to try to understand your gut-feeling and (ii) if needs be support your gut-feeling even if they do not have enough real evidence of the reasoning behind it. You may also find it useful to remember Vitamin C (Focus points – Chapter 4).

In trying to unlock the reasons that have led to your 'gut-feeling', maybe use the Johari Window and close members of your support network to try to (i) explore your Blind Spots and Unknown areas, (ii) challenge your explanation, perhaps using the 5 Whys (see Chapter 2) and (iii) test your explanation for logic and justification.

Useful reading: Chapter 3 – Johari Window
Chapter 12 – Followership

This chapter, along with the final chapter, will discuss broader aspects of change with the aim of helping you to:

> better anticipate new changes

> deal with the more intangible issues of impending changes

> consider how you handle change in the broader context of your life away from work.

The chapters may therefore seem more reflective and will challenge you to think outside your comfort zone.

Being able to anticipate situations and changes, plus interpreting the emotional state or mood of others, is a vital skill and, for many, not an easy one to learn. As discussed in Chapter 3 – *Navigating change successfully*, the importance of recognizing other people's preferences, influences and orientations will help you to gain a broader insight into what could be influencing their behaviours. For example, try applying MBTI preferences, considering a person's focus (past, present or future) and taking perceptual positions.

In Figure 13.1 the transition curve has been overlaid with some of the typical states you may observe as someone progresses along it.

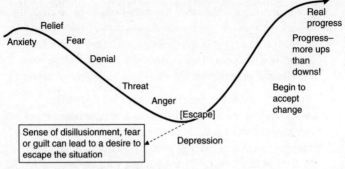

Figure 13.1 Stages on the transition curve

The labels on the figure read:

Anxiety
Relief
Fear
Denial
Threat
Anger
[Escape]

Sense of disillusionment, fear or guilt can lead to a desire to escape the situation

Depression

Real progress
Progress— more ups than downs!
Begin to accept change

Try it now

Without using the transition curve directly, ask some colleagues questions about challenges they are facing and see if you can gauge where they are on their transition curve.

After assessing where they may be, you might like to also consider:

1 What you could do to help them to move forwards along their transition curve.

2 How their current state might be affecting other work or challenges they are facing.

As well as reading signals from the behaviours of those you work with, it can be extremely beneficial to gain awareness and knowledge of what is occurring on the fringes of your world or further afield, i.e. externally. In the military and in espionage they often refer to this as gathering 'intel'. People in Marketing and Sales are often adept at doing this in the commercial world.

Key idea

Consider an aspect of your working life where you could apply the Network Matrix in Figure 13.2 to help you gain 'intel' about things could affect part of your job. No matter whether the role is big or small, look around the organization or externally (e.g. suppliers, customers, industry sectors, technology sectors) to see where and how you could develop your network.

Figure 13.2 shows a model that is extracted from marketing and sales practices for acquiring commercial 'intel' and developing networks. Both aspects offer insights into how you can develop your ability to anticipate change.

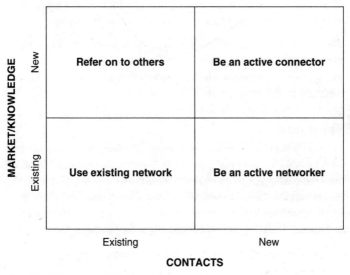

Figure 13.2 The network matrix

Use existing network. This is the safest and most reliable element of networking; however, if you are seeking to broaden your 'intel' then it will most likely produce the most limited results.

Refer on to others. For some this part of networking may mark the beginning of moving slightly out of their comfort zone, in order to make the best use of your existing network and to develop it. The suggestion here is that you consider who in your network could help someone else within your network. Put yourself in the position of being someone who 'connects' people. This principle can then be further expanded as you learn new things about existing contacts or make new contacts and learn about their roles and challenges. For example, if you know that one of your contacts needs help in an area where another of your contacts has knowledge or experience then refer them on.

Be an active networker. As has been already touched on, staying in regular contact with your existing network is very important. Taking this point one step further, consider yourself as a proactive 'networker' and be regularly making new contacts. With new contacts do not forget to consider how they may be useful to others in your network, i.e. refer on to others.

Be an active connector. Perhaps for many people the hardest element of networking is being the conduit to connect other people when you are working in areas that are new to you. Sound strange or difficult?

Try it now

Consider this situation. You are at an external training day where you are with people you have never met before. Seem familiar or uncomfortable? Well the challenge is to try to get to know, briefly, as many people as you can during the day. As you do so look for links between these new contacts, and see if you could help them by making introductions, which in turn could lead to you finding another new useful contact or piece of 'intel'.

You may think that this is not relevant because, for example, you don't need to have much of a network in the job you do. Perhaps ask yourself if you have been in a situation where, by knowing other people in the organization who are from outside your area of work, you might have been able to learn something which would have helped you to deal better with a change, or a piece of work.

Take the story of Helen. She had recently joined a new business as a manager, having moved across from a competitor company in the same sector. Her first task was to assess the capability and competence of her department. As this was Helen's third job in her career, she knew it would be important for her to establish an effective network throughout the company so that she could gain a balanced perspective of her team's performance and needs.

Being from a competitor company, Helen was mindful that, whilst many would welcome her with open arms and seek her knowledge, she needed to be respectful of her network and be aware that there may be some in the new company who would feel threatened by her knowledge.

Firstly Helen created a 30-day, 60-day and 90-day plan and began to map out her new network within the organization. She did this by using an organization chart and taking notes about each person as she got to know them. From this she began to detect that there was a discernible split between two of the key departments that her team relied on.

One of those departments tended to be very reactive and therefore came across as disorganized and, at times, aggressive towards her department. It did appear that they were capable of doing a good job. The second department was more interesting to her as, on the surface, they seemed more considered and open to new ideas. However, more delving into their history showed that there was a tribal element to how they operated and they could be very slow if they did not favour the changes or ideas being proposed.

Helen decided to test her thinking and prepare her thoughts on the capability of her department. She wanted to identify solutions for the future which were achievable yet challenging. This would mean using her external network as well as rapidly expanding her internal network to gain different perspectives, so that she could ensure her report would be widely accepted.

In order to do this Helen used the networking matrix, plus Time Line phases (past, present and future – see below), along with the MAC model discussed on the following page that highlights managing and anticipating change.

Remember this

In order to produce a well-rounded opinion of another department, you need to gain wider 'intel' that may enable you to better anticipate where there may be resistance or allies in future. Try to gain clarity of the areas where you can gain influence as well as control. Chapter 12 provides more information on this.

The MAC model (Managing and Anticipating Change) illustrates four stages people often go through as they make the transition from learning of a change they will be involved in, to accepting within themselves their role in the change.

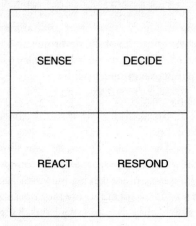

SENSE	DECIDE
REACT	RESPOND

Figure 13.3 The MAC model – Phase 1

In the MAC model, the first stage of Phase 1, above, is about 'sensing' that a change is to occur. Key to sensing early, rather than being surprised, is to develop acuity, i.e. the ability to notice a number of seemingly unrelated details that together add up to a conclusion which may not otherwise be immediately obvious. This may be a combination of seeing, hearing and feeling. If someone senses but takes no action then this invariably is the first step towards denial.

However, those who actively sense will be more inclined to begin assessing what they have noticed and will seek to calibrate their first impressions with other sources of data, just as Helen did in the case study above. She used the combination of facts, opinions and her gut-feeling to form a judgement about the competence of her team.

Stage Two is about how you react to your initial feelings and possibly the assessments that you make. Typically, if the reaction is quick, the likelihood is that it is emotionally driven.

Stage Three is where you try to apply logical thinking to the information you have sensed and the reactions that have occurred; be they your own or those of others. Often included in this stage is the assessment you make of the others involved in the situation, which is better done once you have your emotions under control.

Stage Four is the conclusion of the first three and hopefully where you are able to make a good decision based on reliable information blended occasionally with appropriate 'gut-feelings'. The second aspect of this stage is the choice to not walk away from a decision, but rather to stay in touch with it in case an adaptation needs to be made.

In Phase 2 of the MAC model, below, the additional aspect 'Manage' has been included, and represents the control loop which is required to enable you to continually assess each stage.

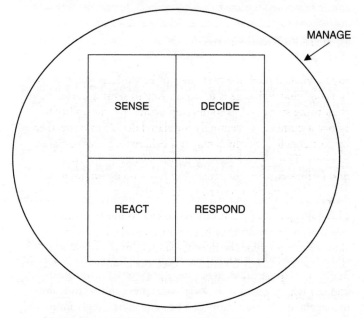

Figure 13.4 The MAC model – Phase 2

If we consider the previous case study, Helen used the 'Manage' control loop to assess the information (factual and sensory) which she was receiving, along with the Time Line model (below), to try to achieve a balanced perspective of the current situation so she could then project forward to decide on the next step. The Time Line model uses three phases to consider past, present and future:

▶ Past – to gain value from previous experience (hers and others)

▶ Present – to contrast and compare with what was currently happening

▶ Future – to evaluate the viability of her aims and objectives, and assess what adjustments she may need to make to her thinking, behaviour and plans.

Remember this

Using the Time Line model above, people with busy lives can make the time to reflect, and use any knowledge or 'intel', to consider both what may happen in the future and how they might deal with future events. Remember the suggestion made in Chapter 12 of having a sanctuary, which could be a good place in which to reflect.

There is an additional aspect within the MAC model which can impact on the decision making stage. As discussed in this book, our moods or the moods of others provide an example of the emotional distortion which directly influences the quality of our decision making. In the model shown in Figure 13.5 emotional distortion can cause the first three stages to become disconnected. The result is that our decision making becomes inconsistent, which in turn means managing change can become very difficult.

So being able to manage our emotions effectively is vital. This concept is called Emotional Intelligence (Bradberry and Greaves, 2009). Emotional Intelligence incorporates self awareness and self management plus social awareness and relationship management. These factors can become increasingly more significant as you progress into senior positions within an organization.

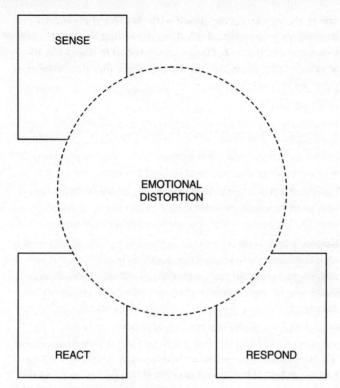

Figure 13.5 Emotional distortion and decision making

EMOTIONAL INTELLIGENCE

▶ **Self awareness** is your ability to accurately assess your emotions and understand your tendencies.

▶ **Self management** is your ability to assess your emotions and select the appropriate things to say and do.

▶ **Social awareness** is your ability to sense and correctly translate the emotions of others.

▶ **Relationship management** is your ability to combine the previous three factors to give clear communications without conflict. If conflict is required then you are able to deal with it sensitively and effectively.

Having a high level of emotional intelligence will enable individuals to stop and think before reacting. With low levels of emotional intelligence, people tend to react first and think later, which can often lead to outbursts or inappropriate behaviour.

Focus points

Networking – try not to regard networking as a necessary evil. Better to recognize it as an important source of information that can help you to develop yourself, your public perception and enhance your ability to anticipate change and be a useful resource to others.

Peripheral vision – no matter how busy you are always keep using all your senses to assess the world around you, so pay equal attention to what you see, hear and feel. Also maintain a healthy curiosity.

Balance – while there is much to consider and try to apply and improve on, it is important to pay attention to your mind and body. If either of them starts to underperform then things will become much more challenging for you. As with juggling, it is vital to keep everything in balance.

Interpreting – it is often said that 'perception is greater than truth', nonetheless it is important that you remain authentic and keep asking questions to test assumptions you may be making, or others may be making of you. Similarly you cannot simply rely on facts so sometimes you need to make interpretations from limited information. Hence be alert to what you are sensing and rationalizing. Your feelings can really help you to make good interpretations of what is happening around you.

Landscape – Following on from all the previous four points, it is very important to ensure you are considering things in the right context, i.e. the emotional climate and background to the situation.

Next steps

The final chapter looks beyond work and considers how the concepts in this book could be applied in the broader context of personal life, exploring the wider benefits available.

Applying change principles in life

In this chapter you will learn:

- ▶ *About handling change in your broader life away from work*
- ▶ *How to achieve a good life–work balance*
- ▶ *How to use change to create new outcomes*
- ▶ *About supporting others with their changes*

Self-assessment

Think of your current situation and answer the following questions:

1 What motivates you more – work or life?

2 How quickly do you bounce back from a change at work, or a change in life?

3 What are the types of changes that you give most attention to?

4 What are your three greatest accomplishments to date?

5 What made them stand out for you?

6 How could you use what you have learned from these accomplishments to assist you in making future changes?

7 What would you like to change in your life?

8 Imagine that you could change just one thing in your life. What would it be?

9 What is stopping you from doing it?

10 What is one action you can take to get started?

Answers

1 Some people live to work, and others work to live. In essence it means that some of us are driven by our work, and our satisfaction and sense of meaning is derived from this source. For other people, they view work as a means to an end and a way of making enough money to enjoy their life outside work to the full. It is critical to understand whether you are fundamentally a 'live to work' or a 'work to live' type person. This will allow you to develop realistic expectations about yourself, and to choose career paths and employers accordingly. For the most part, high achievers who excel in demanding careers are people who live to work.

2 Developing resilience is a fundamental process that can help with change both in work and life. This is the ability to bounce back to normal functioning after a stressful event. The American Psychological Association suggests '10 Ways to Build Resilience' which are highlighted below:

- ▶ maintain good relationships with close family members, friends and others

- ▶ avoid seeing crises or stressful events as unbearable problems

- ▶ accept circumstances that cannot be changed

- ▶ develop realistic goals and move towards them

- ▶ take decisive actions in adverse situations

- ▶ look for opportunities of self-discovery after a struggle with loss

- ▶ develop self-confidence

- ▶ keep a long term perspective and consider the stressful event in a broader context

- ▶ maintain a hopeful outlook, expecting good things and visualizing what is wished for

- ▶ take care of one's mind and body, exercising regularly, paying attention to one's own needs and feelings and engaging in relaxing activities that one enjoys.

All of these actions will help an individual to bounce back more quickly from a change situation regardless of whether it is at work or in life.

3 Think about the types of changes that you focus on. This may give you a clue as to any subconscious preferences that you have, and where your area of comfort may lie. For example, if you notice changes that relate to electronics or mechanical devices it may demonstrate that you have a particular interest in that area. Some people may immediately notice changes that other people make to their hairstyle or clothing, whereas for others it passes them by. Another area to think about is what do you often find most frustrating in others and wish they would change? Often what you tend to notice in others is what you most need to change about yourself! For example, if you always notice that other people seem to be so organized, and you find it frustrating, it may be that you need to change and be more organized!

4 By writing down your three greatest accomplishments you can begin to focus on successes in your life to date. Too often people are quick to notice things that have not worked out as they might have wanted them to, rather than acknowledge successes.

5 If you understand what made them stand out, you get beneath your own motivation, and notice the values or beliefs that are really important to you. The 5 Whys exercise in Chapter 2 can help in this process. This will also be highlighted later in this chapter, using the neurological levels of change model.

6 Many people do not immediately translate successes they have achieved in different areas of their lives across to an immediate problem. For example, a woman who has been out of the workforce whilst bringing up children may not view that experience as a success when thinking about finding a new job. However, if she considered that the skills she used included project management, negotiation, planning, influencing and motivating, she may be able to apply that knowledge in another area of her life or work. Taking time out to reflect and consider situations that you have dealt with which you may not have thought were directly relevant is a useful exercise, and will help in gaining motivation for change in a different area of your work or life.

7 If you could wave a magic wand and change your life – what would you want to change? For some people they can immediately come up with a long list of improvements whereas others struggle. The Johari Window described in Chapter 3 is a tool that shows how seeking feedback from others and being prepared to disclose information about yourself to others, can help you explore areas of hidden potential. Remember that even if you want to stay the same it will require some type of change to make that happen. An exercise that can help you focus on the future outcome rather than 'how' you make it happen is to write a letter to yourself from the future. This will be explained more fully later in this chapter.

8 If you know which area of your life you want to change first, it gives you a sense of focus. Often people know something needs to change but they are unsure as to how to move forwards and take some action. Many of the tools described in this book are equally as useful in life changes as they are for work changes. Prioritizing forces you to work on only one change at a time and see meaningful progress which will keep you motivated.

9 Resistance to change is a key part of the process that has been discussed in each chapter so far and often occurs when the person instigating the change at work has not involved people or clearly communicated the reason for the change. However, resistance to change in your life is slightly different because this time YOU are in control. If you have tried to make changes before and they have not worked out, it can impact on self-esteem and confidence, and can put you off taking similar steps again. There is a presupposition that is used in the field of neurolinguistic programming which is 'there is no failure only feedback'. Take the example of two boys learning to ride a bicycle. Boy A keeps falling off and saying to himself, 'This is hard, I can't do it, maybe I am a failure.' And eventually he thinks this so often he is reluctant to try again. On the other hand, Boy B keeps falling off and he says to himself, 'Wow, these last two times I think I was not holding on correctly and then this time I was one handed; perhaps if I hold on tight and look ahead that might help me improve.' He keeps going and sees his experience as learning, and therefore is happy to keep trying new things and learning and improving. So think about what you are telling yourself when trying to make changes – are you thinking failure or learning?

10 When making a change in life, take one step at a time. Review progress (as learning!) and it is likely to give you the motivation for your next action. Expect that there will be obstacles and setbacks along the way and, by developing resilience, as described in question 2, you can keep on the path to making improvements.

WHICH AREAS TO CHANGE?

Many people are not happy with their life yet are reluctant to make significant changes. However, if you have read the previous chapters in this book, which provide you with many

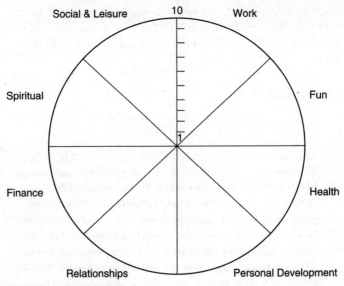

Figure 14.1 The Wheel of Life

tools and techniques to help cope with change at work, these tools can also be applied to your personal life.

The diagram in Figure 14.1 is often referred to as the Wheel of Life. It can help you to focus on areas of your life where you are already happy and to identify others that you would like to change. Consider each area and mark it with a score of 1 (lowest) – 10 (highest) and ask yourself the following questions:

1 Which areas score the highest?

2 What is the reason for this?

3 Which areas are scoring lower than others?

4 What is the impact of this?

5 Am I deliberately choosing my life to be balanced the way it currently is?

6 How would I like it to be different in three months, six months, one year?

7 What will be my first steps to making this happen?

Use the wheel to work out how you would like your life to be. Each area does not have to be in balance with the others as long as you have consciously identified that you want it to be that way.

Try it now

Carry out the Wheel of Life exercise in order to identify which areas you would like to change. Create your own action plan for the next 12 months.

One way to consider it is like a graphic equalizer which is designed to balance all the bass and treble frequencies in a music signal. If you put them all at zero, you might have them balanced appropriately for jazz music but when playing pop or classical, it will not sound as good as it could do. So to gain the optimum sound you consciously choose how to adapt each element for the situation.

In life it is a similar concept. Some people will consciously choose to be out of balance and focus on one area of their life that they are passionate about. Take the story of Rebecca as an example. She was a talented athlete and from the age of 15 was training at the athletics track three nights a week along with her coach. She began to win races and really enjoyed the longer distance races, especially the 5000 m which demanded a lot of endurance training.

Rebecca decided she really wanted to find out what her capabilities were and so devoted all her time to athletics. As a result, sport dominated her life and most of her friends were involved in athletics too. This was ideal until Rebecca was injured and she was not able to run for almost a year. All of a sudden Rebecca realized she had been so focused on sport that she had no other interests, and she did not really want to be around her friends who were talking about their latest race results when she was not able to do any running at all.

The risk that Rebecca had taken to see what she could achieve as an athlete was now showing the downsides. It was a tough year for Rebecca as she had to regain some more balance in her life and develop new interests and friends outside sport.

Remember this

When you make a conscious choice to focus on different elements in your life, make sure you consider the risks of putting all your energies into those activities, as well as the benefits to be gained. That way you can make an educated choice about how you want the balance to be. Some will consider work and life balance to be like a see-saw – it has to be evenly balanced – while others will view it as proportional, say 80 per cent work and 20 per cent life etc.

Once you have decided which areas you wish to change, it is important to identify the outcome you want to achieve as a result. This will help you to gain commitment to the change as you move around the change curve.

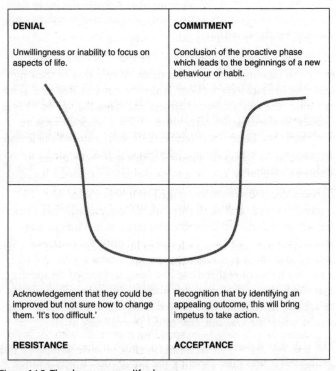

Figure 14.2 The change curve – life changes

By now you will have learned more about your personality preferences if you have carried out the assessments described in Chapters 3 (Myers-Briggs Type Indicator® and past, present, future focus); Chapter 7 (Belbin team types) and Chapter 8 (DISC). This will help you to have a better idea of how you behave in various situations. You can use this knowledge to create the type of outcome that will help motivate you to change.

One method is to write yourself a letter from the future. This will help you create the possibilities for a brighter, improved future. Your brain does not distinguish between thoughts about real situations and imaginary ones, so the clearer you make your future in the letter, the more real it will become in your mind.

Take the story of Gary as an example. He had worked in an insurance company for most of his career. He was 42 years old and had a wife and two children. Gary was driven by the need for achievement and measured his success in terms of his salary and the recognition he received from his friends and colleagues. Once he got to grips with a job, he immediately began looking for the next step up the ladder, which generally meant longer hours, more travel and less time at home or socializing. However, he was driven to keep striving for the next big job.

Eventually, he began to question if this was really going to make him happy in the long term and talked through his frustrations with his wife. They agreed that in order for him to have a better quality of life, less stress and more happiness, things would have to change.

Gary sat down and wrote a letter to himself describing how he would like life to be in two years' time.

> Now two years on I am pleased to say that I feel happier with myself, and my life. Rather than rushing from one job to the next, I am enjoying the 'here and now' and as a consequence have been spending more time with my wife and family. It feels like a much closer family unit now, and my children have gained from my support and attention.

Although work is still important to me, it is no longer the dominant factor in my life. I now recognize the importance of doing what I want rather than living up to the expectations of others.

I have consciously slowed down and taken more time to reflect and take satisfaction from what I have already achieved. This is not to say I have become complacent. Instead I focus on aspects of my work that I can influence and control, which has removed a lot of stress from my life.

Whilst Gary had no idea how this would become a reality when he wrote the letter, he found that it made a difference and subconsciously he changed his focus and accepted that he needed to change.

Try it now

Create an appealing outcome by writing yourself a letter from the future. Include what you will see, hear and feel at a specific time in the future. Make sure you write in 'present' language, i.e. I am doing this, as opposed to future language, i.e. I will be doing this. If writing does not appeal to you, then draw a picture using bright colours and images to denote how life is at that time in the future.

For people who prefer detail (see Myers-Briggs preferences in Chapter 3) there is the option to create milestones in between where you are today and the outcome in the letter or picture. However, rather than plotting the milestones from the perspective of the present, it can be more enlightening to review them from the future and then take a journey backwards from the future to the present day.

This can be done by carrying out the exercise below:

Creating your Future

1   Decide the future changes that you want by writing a letter or drawing a picture. Identify the current situation that you are in today. (NOW)

2 Draw an imaginary line on the floor, decide on a start point for NOW and an end point for the moment when the outcome has been successfully achieved. (FUTURE NOW)

3 Stand at the NOW point and notice the present situation.

4 Stand at FUTURE NOW when the outcome has been successfully achieved and look back at NOW. Think about what you see, what you hear and what you feel at the moment in time when you have achieved your outcome. Describe it in the present tense: *I see myself smiling and laughing, I feel proud and relieved, etc.*

5 Look back towards NOW and notice how the events along the line realign themselves in the light of having achieved that outcome. Look back along the timeline and notice any difficult point or obstacles. Notice the milestones that have inserted themselves.

6 From that FUTURE NOW give your old self advice. Now walk slowly back along the line from FUTURE NOW to NOW, paying attention to any thoughts that spring to mind.

7 Write down any new ideas, thoughts and actions that you need to take.

This exercise should help you to identify the obstacles that might get in the way. Another method of considering these could be to have a chat with someone you know well and whose advice you trust. Tell them about what you want your future to be like and ask them what obstacles they think could arise.

This brings to life the concept of the Learning Ladder described in Chapter 8 and enables you to think ahead and anticipate changes rather than waiting for them to happen to you. More details about anticipating change are also described in Chapter 13. However, for those who remain firmly in the resistance element of the change curve and do not move to acceptance, there may be another way to get insight into what is stopping them.

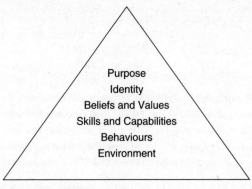

Figure 14.3 Neurological levels of change

The neurological levels of change (Figure 14.3) are very useful for assisting with or understanding change from an individual point of view. They were developed by Robert Dilts and are based on the 'neurological levels' proposed by anthropologist Gregory Bateson. Making a change at a lower level (i.e. environment) may, but not necessarily, affect an upper level. However, a change at an upper level (i.e. belief) will have a distinct impact on the levels below it.

Take the story of Chloe. In her spare time, she wanted to write a book on dog training, which was her passion. So she decided that the best place to write was in the library, where the peace and quiet would help her concentrate. Every day she went down to the library and tried to write. But nothing happened, she just stared at the paper and no words came to mind.

When an individual embarks on making a change and it's not working, the first thing they may do is change the **Environment.** So Chloe decided that maybe the library was too quiet and so she moved her location to the coffee shop, hoping that this would bring new inspiration. However, the problem remained that Chloe was stuck on how to start writing the book.

Her next change was to her **Behaviour**. Chloe knew she was most energetic in the morning, so for the next week she arrived in the coffee shop at 9 a.m. which allowed her two hours a day to write. But it was hard and by the end of the week, she had little to show for her efforts.

Chloe's next plan was to change her **Skills and Capabilities** and that meant going on a writing course. So, having paid for a weekend course in the hope that it would help her to get going, she found herself the following week back at the café, and nothing had changed. Often it is at this stage that many thousands of pounds are spent in organizations around the world on training courses that people attend and then go back to work and nothing changes. Why?

Because the answer is not to change the Environment, Behaviours or Skills, but somewhere in the upper three levels of the model, i.e. **Beliefs and Values**, **Identity** and **Purpose**. Chloe realized she did not actually believe she could be a writer and this was holding her back. She also never imagined that she would ever describe herself as an author, and this too was stopping her. And the highest level is **Purpose**, and what we see as our role 'here on earth'. Using the model in Figure 14.3 can help you to identify what is 'really stopping you' from changing. If you review question 9 at the start of this chapter, it is now clear that Boy A had a self-limiting belief about 'I am a failure' which did not enable him to learn to ride a bicycle.

Level	Questions to ask yourself
Purpose	This is considering the fundamental questions Why are you here? What is your purpose?
Identity	Who? Who are you as an individual? What role do you play to achieve your purpose? How do you think of yourself as a person – e.g. 'I am a successful businesswoman'.
Beliefs and Values	Why? Values are the rules that you live your life by. Understanding what is important to you as an individual and what drives you will have an impact on how you behave.
Skills and Capabilities	How? How do you go about doing things? As an individual, what are your capabilities, skills, strategies or action plans?
Behaviours	What? What behaviours need to change?
Environment	Where? What environmental factors influence the change?

Try it now

When you sense resistance to change, ask yourself, 'What is REALLY stopping me?' Then review the logical levels model and think about at which level you really need to make the change which will impact on all the lower levels.

Once the obstacles to commitment have been removed then you are able to focus on taking the actions required to make changes in your life. It takes up to 28 days to create a new habit so any actions have to be continued for at least a month.

Remember this

Change because it will improve your life or work, not just because it is the fashion.

SUPPORTING OTHERS IN CHANGE

Other people you know may also want to (or need to) make changes to parts of their life and you are now in a position to help them. Notice which stage of the change curve they may be at, and think about how you could be a useful support to them. If they are in denial or resistance, it's no use pushing them because it can often make them dig their heels in more.

However, use the power of curiosity to ask them questions, which will help to raise their awareness about their current situation.

THE GROW MODEL

The GROW model, originally conceived by Graham Alexander and brought to prominence by Sir John Whitmore, is possibly the best-known model for coaching. Whitmore made his name in the field of high performance coaching in the sporting arena, but the technique is flexible enough to be applied virtually anywhere. Like most models it provides a structure for the coaching conversation and is designed to ensure some form of action towards an outcome.

▶ G – GOAL

Ask questions to help the person identify what they want to achieve.

What do you want to achieve?

▶ R – REALITY

Help them understand what is actually going on rather than working on assumptions or only through their perceptions.

What is really going on?

▶ O – OPTIONS

This stage of the process is to explore the possible options of behaviour or decisions that will help them move forwards.

What could you do?

▶ W – WILL

The final stage is used to ask questions related to what specific actions will the person take to move towards their stated goal.

What will you do?

The structure of the GROW model is a good starting point to help others through change. It is worth recognizing that often most people will not start a conversation by stating a goal but by talking about reality, so if you are going to help them, begin with reality and then move them up to the GOAL part of the model, which will help them get clarity and focus. A similar model that also helps to provide clarity of thinking in a change situation is C L E A R (Contract, Listen, Explore, Action, Review), developed by Peter Hawkins of the Bath Consultancy Group.

If you have now identified the stage of change that your colleague or friend is at, then storytelling can be used as a way of inspiring change. Whilst no one wants to be told '*What*

I think you should do is...', a story that describes a similar experience and how it was resolved leaves the door open for the listener to form their own judgement without feeling pushed into action.

MAINTAINING COMMITMENT

Once you have either identified an action for you to take, or you have helped someone else to do so, then the next important factor is how to maintain commitment and stay on track.

It can be fairly difficult to remain committed to a new way of working or behaving, particularly if you have little support from others. In Chapter 10 there is mention of the process of developing resilience, which is also reinforced in question 2 in this chapter, as a way of bouncing back when things go wrong or not as expected.

Factors that help you to remain committed to your goals	Factors that can get in the way of your being committed to your goals
Support from others	Health and wellbeing
Having the goal defined in sufficient detail to provide clarity	Misuse of time, e.g. distractions
	Goal is too vague or too big
Measuring progress	Mindset, e.g. 'I am a failure'
Seeing regular progress	Insufficient or inappropriate support
Self-belief	You get sidetracked by a new interest that you perceive is better or more attractive to spend time on
Passion	
Tenacity	
Resilience	Propensity to 'give up'

Try it now

Review the table above, and you will notice that most of the factors are 'internal', which means you are in control of them, as opposed to external factors that you have little or no influence over.

Therefore, being aware of what you say to yourself, i.e. 'self-talk', can help to highlight the messages that you are communicating to yourself, sometimes without realizing it. For example, some phrases that individuals say to themselves are:

'I always do… when things get tough…' which can be challenged by rephrasing to 'I used to do…and this time I will do…(something different)…'.

'It's too hard, I can't do it' which can be restated as 'I will give it a try, and I recognize there may be challenges along the way'.

So be aware that you may sabotage your own progress by what you say to yourself internally. Similarly become aware of what you are noticing, and make sure you acknowledge progress and successes, rather than only just what is not working as you hoped. For example Mary was a stressed out executive working in a large corporate. She decided to make a commitment to start swimming twice a week in a bid to keep fit. However, at the end of the first month she had reviewed progress and, rather than recognizing that she had been swimming four times in the month, she felt bad because she had only managed to get to the pool once a week rather than twice.

Once Mary became aware that she was sabotaging her own goals, she chose to only focus on progress, rather than what she had set out to do and not accomplished. The original goal she had set herself was perhaps too optimistic, and therefore Mary was getting a skewed view of progress because it was not viable in the first place. In reality Mary was progressing because she had actually begun to do more exercise than previously.

Remember this

If you could do just one thing, what would it be? Notice the successes you achieve, and recognize progress.

Overall, if you want to apply change principles in life then make sure you recognize that the process will be broadly the same, i.e. denial, resistance, acceptance and commitment.

Focus points

Select the areas of your life that you want to change.

Develop a future focused outcome that inspires you to achieve it.

Set goals or milestones that will help you to mark out the route.

If there are obstacles, use the logical levels model to identify where the resistance is.

Help your colleagues and friends to change by using curiosity to ask questions, the GROW model to structure a conversation and storytelling to inspire.

When commitment to action seems challenging, review your self-talk and measure progress to keep you motivated.

By taking one action at a time, you create momentum for change.

Summary

In this book, you will have learned how to cope with different change scenarios at work, by taking personal responsibility and focusing on what you can control and have influence over, rather than feeling that change is 'being done to you'. The tools that are outlined in all the chapters can be applied to life changes as well as work changes.

It is important to remember that change is unavoidable: even if you don't want to, you will change. So being able to recognize it, anticipate it, cope with it and thrive on it will help you to achieve more, get less stressed and enjoy work and life with new insight.

Taking it further

Bradberry, Travis, and Greaves, Jean, *Emotional Intelligence 2.0* (Talent Smart, 2009)

Covey, Stephen, *Seven Habits of Highly Effective People* (Simon and Schuster, 2004)

Echeverría, Rafael, *On Moods and Emotions* (The Newfield Group, 1990)

Firth, Sue, *More Life, Less Stress* (2nd edn, London: Whealth, 2009)

Ibarra, H., Carter, N. M. and Silva, C., 'Why men still get more promotions than women', *Harvard Business Review*, Sept 2010

Karpman, Stephen B., 'Fairy tales and script drama analysis', *Transactional Analysis Bulletin*, Vol 7, No. 26, April 1968

Index